SpringerBriefs in Law

More information about this series at http://www.springer.com/series/10164

Sergio Carrera

Implementation of EU Readmission Agreements

Identity Determination Dilemmas and the Blurring of Rights

Sergio Carrera
Justice and Home Affairs Research
   Programme
CEPS
Brussels
Belgium

ISSN 2192-855X　　　　　　　ISSN 2192-8568　(electronic)
SpringerBriefs in Law
ISBN 978-3-319-42504-7　　　ISBN 978-3-319-42505-4　(eBook)
DOI 10.1007/978-3-319-42505-4

Library of Congress Control Number: 2016945141

© The Editor(s) (if applicable) and The Author(s) 2016. This book is published open access.
Open Access This book is distributed under the terms of the Creative Commons Attribution 4.0 International License (http://creativecommons.org/licenses/by/4.0/), which permits use, duplication, adaptation, distribution and reproduction in any medium or format, as long as you give appropriate credit to the original author(s) and the source, a link is provided to the Creative Commons license and any changes made are indicated.
The images or other third party material in this book are included in the work's Creative Commons license, unless indicated otherwise in the credit line; if such material is not included in the work's Creative Commons license and the respective action is not permitted by statutory regulation, users will need to obtain permission from the license holder to duplicate, adapt or reproduce the material.
The use of general descriptive names, registered names, trademarks, service marks, etc. in this publication does not imply, even in the absence of a specific statement, that such names are exempt from the relevant protective laws and regulations and therefore free for general use.
The publisher, the authors and the editors are safe to assume that the advice and information in this book are believed to be true and accurate at the date of publication. Neither the publisher nor the authors or the editors give a warranty, express or implied, with respect to the material contained herein or for any errors or omissions that may have been made.

Printed on acid-free paper

This Springer imprint is published by Springer Nature
The registered company is Springer International Publishing AG Switzerland

Endorsements

As the drive for readmission is steadily gaining momentum in European policy discourses and practices, together with its repeated calls for "effectiveness", this comparative study is, to say the least, timely and necessary. It is timely because never before has the readmission mantra been so pervasive and constant in European policy-making. It is necessary because all the democratic challenges, as well as the myths, surrounding the concrete implementation of EU and bilateral readmission agreements need to be critically addressed and disclosed. Anyone interested in understanding will find much in this study to stimulate a reflection on issues of high political and societal relevance. Sergio Carrera's reflection accurately captures the unsaid tensions between states' international human rights obligations and their declared intention to accelerate the removal of irregular foreigners. This is a must read for researchers and practitioners alike.

Jean-Pierre Cassarino
Institut de Recherche sur le Maghreb Contemporain
Author of "Unbalanced Reciprocities"

This book convincingly shows that the growing emphasis on expelling migrants sets the risk of overlooking or ignoring the practical consequences and, eventually, fundamental human rights effects of these policies. Carrera had succeeded in connecting the political context of EURAs with the implementation challenges on the ground, including the judicial scrutiny of the expulsion practices. This comprehensive assessment reveals conclusions on the effectiveness of the EURAs that were not drawn in previous scholarly contributions. Carrera's analysis reads as an urgent appeal to reconsider the EU return and readmission policy by reconciling it with the individuals' fundamental rights.

Tineke Strik
Parliamentary Assembly of the Council of Europe (PACE) and
Centre for Migration Law (Radboud University of Nijmegen)

Acknowledgments

This book falls within the scope of the EURA-NET (*Transnational Migration in Transition*) research project which is funded by the Seventh Framework Programme of DG Research of the European Commission. For more information about the project, refer to http://www.uta.fi/edu/en/research/projects/eura-net/index.html.

The author would like to express his gratitude to Prof. Elspeth Guild (Queen Mary London University, Radboud University of Nijmegen and CEPS) for her insights and comments on a previous version of this manuscript. He would also like to thank Prof. G.R. de Groot (Faculty of Law, Maastricht University), Dr. Natasja Reslow (Faculty of Law, Maastricht University) and Dr. Jean-Pierre Cassarino (*Institut de Recherche sur le Maghreb Contemporain*) for their comments. The author is grateful to Ms. Anne Harrington (editor at CEPS) for proofreading and editing a previous drafted version of this book. He would also like to thank all the EU policy-makers who kindly agreed to be interviewed for the purposes of this research. A preliminary version of this book was presented at the Conference 'Multilayered Governance: Gains for International Migration?' organised under the 'nccr—on the move' project the 27 and 28 May 2016 at the University of Bern (Switzerland). The author would like to express his gratitude to Marion Panizzon and Philip Hanke for their invitation to participate in this Conference, as well as for their comments and those of the discussants and participants. The views expressed are attributable only to the author in a personal capacity and not to any institution with which he is associated.

Contents

1 Introduction 1
   References 5
2 The EU and the Ineffectiveness of Expulsion Policies 7
   References 12
3 Identity Determination Dilemmas: Whose National Are You? 13
   3.1 The Quasi-suspension of the EURA with Pakistan 16
   3.2 Pham v. Secretary of State for the Home Department Case .. 19
   References 21
4 EURAs Compared 23
   4.1 Readmission Obligation of Own Nationals 25
   4.2 Readmission Procedures: Principles and Means of Evidence .. 29
      4.2.1 Principles 29
      4.2.2 Means of Evidence of Nationality 30
      4.2.3 Application and Implementation 33
   References 35
5 The Implementation Challenges and Dynamics of EURAs 37
   5.1 Lack of Accountability and Transparency 37
   5.2 The Value Added of Formal and Informal EU Readmission
      Instruments 42
   5.3 Inter-state and Inter-actor Challenges: Re-modelling
      the Boundaries of Authority 47
   5.4 The Blurring of Rights 52
   References 59
6 Conclusions 63
   References 66
Annex 67

About the Author

Dr. Sergio Carrera is a senior research fellow and head of Justice and Home Affairs Programme, CEPS. He is an associate professor/senior research fellow at the Faculty of Law in Maastricht University (the Netherlands). Carrera is also an honorary professor at the School of Law in Queen Mary University of London (UK). Carrera has authored and coedited several volumes and numerous academic articles in national and international scientific (peer-reviewed) journals. His main research interests are on EU justice and home affairs (JHA) law and policy, with a particular focus on migration, citizenship and border policies. He has been an external expert and written numerous studies for the European Commission, European Parliament, the European Economic and Social Committee, the EU Fundamental Rights Agency and the Committee of the Regions.

Abbreviations

ACP	African, Caribbean and Pacific
AFIS	Automated Fingerprinting Identification System
CJEU	Court of Justice of the European Union
CLS	Council Legal Service
DG	Directorate General
EASO	European Asylum Support Office
EC	European Community
ECHR	European Convention for the Protection of Human Rights and Fundamental Freedoms
EEAS	European External Action Service
EMN	European Migration Network
EU	European Union
EURA	European Union Readmission Agreement
FRA	European Union Agency for Fundamental Rights
IAMAS	Entry-Exit and Registration Automated Information System of the Republic of Azerbaijan
ICCPR	International Covenant on Civil and Political Rights
IT	Information Technology
JRC	Joint Readmission Committee
LIBE	Civil Liberties, Justice and Home Affairs Committee of the European Parliament
MEP	Member of the European Parliament
MoU	Memorandum of Understanding
PAC	Partnership and Cooperation Agreement
PACE	Parliamentary Assembly of the Council of Europe
RA	Readmission Agreement
SIAC	UK Special Immigration Appeals Commission
SIS II	Schengen Information System II
STLD	Interpol Stolen and Lost Travel Documents
TCNs	Third Country Nationals

TFEU	Treaty on the Functioning of the European Union
UK	United Kingdom
UNHCR	UN High Commissioner for Refugees
UNHR	Universal Declaration of Human Rights
VIS	Visa Information System

List of Graphs

Graph 5.1　TCNs subject to the enforcement of immigration legislation in EU. *Source* Eurostat (http://ec.europa.eu/eurostat/statistics-explained/index.php/Statistics_on_enforcement_of_immigration_legislation Accessed 8 June 2016).................................. 38

Graph 5.2　EU member states authorities responsible for implementing EURAs. *Source* Author's own elaboration based on EMN (2014)..................... 39

List of Tables

Table 4.1	EURAs	25
Table 4.2	EURA with Pakistan: documents furnishing nationality or initiating the process of establishing nationality	30
Table 4.3	Documenting legal and functional identity—EURAs compared.	32
Table 5.1	Total number of TCNs ordered to leave and returns EU-28 2008–2014	38
Table 5.2	Total returns and removal orders EU 28 2008–2014 to selected third countries	40
Table 5.3	List of implementing protocols in EURAs	43

Chapter 1
Introduction

One of the key instruments framing cooperation between the European Union (EU) and third countries for purposes of expelling irregular third-country nationals are the EU Readmission Agreements (EURAs). These are international agreements laying down common administrative rules and conditions for the 'readmission' of nationals,[1] third country nationals (TCNs) and stateless persons either to their country of origin or to a country through which they entered or transited on route to the EU. During the last 16 years, and as of May 2016, the EU has concluded 17 EURAs with various non-EU countries.

EURAs constitute a "vital component" in the wider external migration law and policy.[2] Enhancing cooperation with third countries of origin and transit in the field of readmission has been reconfirmed as a policy priority in the external dimensions of the 2015 European Migration Agenda[3] and the subsequent EU Action Plan on Return.[4] Readmission is officially framed as an 'essential' instrument in increasing return and ensuring the success of EU expulsions policies. The European Commission argues that current expulsion systems are 'ineffective', based on the rates of successful returns of third-country nationals issued a removal order.

---

[1] According to the Oxford English Dictionary Online the notion of 'Readmission' means: to readmit/'Readmit': to admit again. The European Commission defined 'readmission' as follows "Act by a state accepting the re-entry of an individual (own nationals, third-country nationals or stateless persons), who has been found illegally entering to, being present in or residing in another state" (European Commission 2002, Annex). The Communication distinguished 'readmission' from 'return' and 'expulsion'. Return was defined as "Comprises the process of going back to one's country of origin, transit or another third country, including preparation and implementation. The return may be voluntary or enforced." The notion of 'expulsion' comprised "Administrative or judicial act, which states—where applicable—the illegality of the entry, stay or residence or terminates the legality of a previous lawful residence e.g. in case of criminal offences."

[2] The Council of the EU has reiterated since early 2000s that cooperation with third countries on return and readmission policy is an integral and vital component in the fight against illegal immigration. Council of the EU (2002a, b).

[3] European Commission (2015a).

[4] European Commission (2015b).

EURAs are deemed to play a key role in increasing the enforcement of removal orders of irregular immigrants. Contrary to their intended goal, it is unclear what value the EURAs contribute in facilitating or increasing the expulsion rates of irregular migrants. Little is known about their operability, uses and effects on the ground.

The adoption and practical implementation of EURAs have faced a series of multi-faceted challenges and criticism of their effectiveness as a tool in the management of migration. EU policy documents have consistently highlighted the obstacles that have impeded the negotiations of EURAs. The academic literature has deeply examined the origins of these legal competence dilemmas and challenges to the rights of both asylum-seekers and refugees and their difficult cohabitation with formal and informal bilateral readmission arrangements with third countries.[5] The scholarly discussion has also focused on the place of EURAs in the so-called 'external dimensions of EU migration policies', and the development of accompanying incentives and conditions by the EU in light of third-country hesitation or lack of interest to cooperate on readmission deals with the Union.[6] Less attention has been paid to the actual reasons why people cannot be expelled in the scope of 'readmission' practices, in particular when it comes to own nationals of the third countries concerned, and what do the most relevant practical and legal barriers behind the implementation of already concluded EURAs tell us about the legitimacy and value added of EU readmission policy.

EURAs generally lay down common operational procedures and administrative rules for 'swiftly' identifying 'migrants to be readmitted' and issuing the necessary travel documents (*laissez-passer*) for their expulsion. Still, the "identification of migrants and delivery of travel documents for their return" has been signalled as one of the most common obstacles affecting the operability of EU readmission practices.[7] A fundamental condition for the EURAs expulsion model to be operational is the success in the procedure for determining 'who is the person' found to be irregularly entering or present in the EU's territory and the legality of such an expulsion once that identity is determined in light of EU law and fundamental rights standards. The identification of the nationality of that person represents the fundamental premise for any readmission regime to function. Determining who the person is and her/his identity constitutes the *sine qua non* for unlocking readmission.

EURAs lay down a common list of documents aimed at facilitating the proof or presuming the determination of nationality of the person to be readmitted between the signatory third country and the EU for the purposes of the EURA. Much attention has been paid to the challenges posed by the inclusion of third country nationals and stateless persons transiting these countries clauses in EURAs. Not enough attention

---

[5]Coleman (2009), Cassarino (2007, 2010, 2014), Panizon (2012), Billet (2010), Schiffer (2003), Roig and Huddleston (2007), Bouteillet-Paquet (2003).
[6]Wolf (2014), Trauner and Kruse (2008), Carrera and Hernandez (2011).
[7]European Commission (2015b), p. 7.

has been given in the literature to implementation challenges of EURAs when it comes to own nationals. This is despite the fact that the process of determining the individual's identity has proven to be one of the most controversial aspects in the implementation of EURAs, which we call the identity determination challenge. This challenge is of particular relevance with respect to cooperation with third countries which are not geographically adjacent to an EU Member State. EURAs have foreseen procedures for readmitting those not qualifying as nationals (i.e. TCNs). Yet the main criterion for readmitting TCNs—i.e. irregularly and directly entering EU's territory—will be more difficult or even impossible to meet for countries that are not closely located in the EU's neighbourhood.

This book aims to close that knowledge gap by examining the implementation dynamics and obstacles affecting the readmission of nationals to their countries of origin in the scope of EURAs.[8] There have been several instances where sharp disagreements have emerged between EU Member States and third countries that have concluded a EURA as to whether the persons to be readmitted are own nationals. Why can nationals not be returned to their own state of origin? What is referred to in EU documents as the unwillingness of countries of origin to readmit or repatriate their own nationals often hides a deeper disagreement between the states concerned as to whether the person(s) involved are or are not nationals of the assigned country of origin.

Identifying who is whose national by EU Member States' authorities in the context of readmission opens up a whole series of existential dilemmas: first from the perspective of the sovereignty of third countries of (alleged) origin and the legal

---

[8]An assessment of the scope and implementation of EU Member States (bilateral) readmission policies and instruments with third countries falls outside the scope of this study. The analysis does not either cover the use of so-called 'readmission clauses' which have been introduced in international (mixed) agreements, e.g. Article 13 Cotonou Partnership Agreement (23 June 2000, revised in 2005) between the European Community and ACP (African, Caribbean and Pacific) countries. Article 13.5.c states that "c) The Parties further agree that: (i)—each Member State of the European Union shall accept the return of and readmission of any of its nationals who are illegally present on the territory of an ACP State, at that State's request and without further formalities;—each of the ACP States shall accept the return of and readmission of any of its nationals who are illegally present on the territory of a Member State of the European Union, at that Member State's request and without further formalities. The Member States and the ACP States will provide their nationals with appropriate identity documents for such purposes. In respect of the Member States of the European Union, the obligations in this paragraph apply only in respect of those persons who are to be considered their nationals for the Community purposes in accordance with Declaration No 2 to the Treaty establishing the European Community. In respect of ACP States, the obligations in this paragraph apply only in respect of those persons who are considered as their nationals in accordance with their respective legal system. (ii) at the request of a Party, negotiations shall be initiated with ACP States aiming at concluding in good faith and with due regard for the relevant rules of international law, bilateral agreements governing specific obligations for the readmission and return of their nationals. These agreements shall also cover, if deemed necessary by any of the Parties, arrangements for the readmission of third country nationals and stateless persons. Such agreements will lay down the details about the categories of persons covered by these arrangements as well as the modalities of their readmission and return."

standards laid down in international legal instruments as regards states' powers in determining nationality, and second regarding the agency of the individual as a citizen and as a holder of fundamental human rights. This process raises several important questions: Who is a national of 'whose' country? What are the procedures through which someone's nationality is determined and who is entitled to take that decision in light of international standards? What rights do individuals possess and which ones might prevent the enforcement of an expulsion order?

The outcomes of any identification process in the context of expulsions are in turn intimately linked to other impediments to removal that are related to the set of rights and procedural safeguards ascribed to the administrative status of the person concerned. In fact, these impediments constitute essential rule of law guarantees now formally enshrined in EU citizenship and migration law as well as the EU Charter of Fundamental Rights. They relate to effective remedies against removal decisions, proportionality tests and fundamental rights standards in cases of humanitarian considerations or other personal and family reasons which, irrespective of the individual's identity, *de jure* or *de facto* make her/him 'non-removable' or non-expellable from a given country of residence.

This book argues that the challenges affecting the identification procedures laid down in EURAs reveal one of the 'weakest links' affecting the *effectiveness* of EU readmission policies. First, they pose a profound test to the sovereignty of the third country and international law standards in determining who is a national of which country; and second, they blur individuals' agency as holders of fundamental human rights and freedoms. The understanding of operational effectiveness in readmission policies from the perspective of increasing expulsion rates is inconsistent with international legal standards framing inter-state relations and the rights of individuals subject to expulsion practices.

The book starts by setting the scene in EU readmission policy. Chapter 2 examines the ways in which the European Commission and the Member States currently frame the effectiveness of EU return policies on the basis of 'successful returns' rates, and the policy and legislative initiatives which have been advanced to increase the number of expulsions. Chapter 3 assesses existing knowledge regarding the role played by travel documents and identity determination as obstacles preventing the person to be expelled or readmitted to her/his country of origin. The chapter illustrates the challenges in determining identity on the basis of two recent practical examples: (i) the quasi-suspension of the EURA with Pakistan in light of the so-called 'European Refugee crisis' and (ii) the UK Supreme Court judgment in *Pham v. Secretary of State for the Home Department*.

Chapter 4 studies the administrative procedures and common rules envisaged by EURAs aimed at ensuring a swift identification or 'identity determination' of the nationality of the persons to be readmitted to their country of origin. It focuses on the ways in which nationality is to be determined or presumed in the scope of the 2010 EURA with Pakistan, and compares it with those foreseen in the five EURAs that have been concluded since with Armenia, Azerbaijan, Cape Verde, Georgia, and Turkey. Particular attention is paid to the differences and commonalities between the EURA with Pakistan and the other five EURAs in terms of the norms and documents determining the nationality of the person to be readmitted. Chapter 5 critically analysis the challenges affecting the operability of EURAs. It is argued that these mainly relate to the lack of accountability and transparency mechanisms as well as the dilemmas that they pose to international and European standards in the determination of nationality by states, and the individual as a holder of fundamental human rights.

Open Access This chapter is distributed under the terms of the Creative Commons Attribution 4.0 International License (http://creativecommons.org/licenses/by/4.0/), which permits use, duplication, adaptation, distribution and reproduction in any medium or format, as long as you give appropriate credit to the original author(s) and the source, a link is provided to the Creative Commons license and any changes made are indicated.

The images or other third party material in this chapter are included in the work's Creative Commons license, unless indicated otherwise in the credit line; if such material is not included in the work's Creative Commons license and the respective action is not permitted by statutory regulation, users will need to obtain permission from the license holder to duplicate, adapt or reproduce the material.

References

Billet C (2010) EC readmission agreements: a prime instrument of the external dimension of the EU's fight against irregular immigration: an assessment after ten years of practice. Eur J Migr Law 12:45–79

Bouteillet-Paquet D (2003) Passing the buck: a critical analysis of the readmission policy implemented by the European Union and its member states. Eur J Migr Law 5:359–377

Carrera S and Hernández i Sagrera R (2011) Mobility partnerships: 'Insecurity partnerships' for policy coherence and migrant workers' human rights in the EU. In: Kunz R, Lavanex S and Panizzon M (eds)Multilayered migration governance: The promise of partnership. Routledge, London

Cassarino JP (2007) Informalising readmission agreements in the EU neighbourhood. Int Spectator 42(2):179–196

Cassarino JP (2010) Readmission policy in the European Union. Study for the European Parliament, Brussels

Cassarino JP (2014) A reappraisal of the EU's expanding readmission system. Int Spectator 49 (4):130–145

Coleman N (2009) European readmission policy. Third country interests and refugee rights. Martinus Nijhoff, Leiden

Council of the EU (2002a) Comprehensive plan to combat illegal immigration and trafficking of human beings in the European Union, Brussels, 28 Feb 2002

Council of the EU (2002b) Proposal for a return action programme. 14673/02, Brussels, 25 Nov 2002

European Commission (2002) Communication on the Community return policy on illegal residents. COM (2002) 564 final, 14 Oct 2002

European Commission (2015a) A European agenda on migration. COM (2015) 240, 13 May 2015

European Commission (2015b) Recommendation establishing a common "Return Handbook" to be used by Member States' competent authorities when carrying out return related tasks. C (2015) 6250, 1 Oct 2015

Panizon M (2012) Readmission agreements of EU member states: a case for EU subsidiarity or dualism? Refugee Surv Q 31(4):101–133

Roig A, Huddleston T (2007) EC readmission agreements: a re-evaluation of the political impasse. Eur J Migr Law 9:363–387

Schiffer M (2003) Community readmission agreements with third countries—Objectives, substance and current state of negotiations. Eur J Migr Law 5:343–357

Trauner F, Kruse I (2008) EC visa facilitation and readmission agreements: a new standard EU foreign policy tool? Eur J Migr Law. 10(4):411–438

Wolf S (2014) The politics of negotiating EU readmission agreements: insights from Morocco and Turkey. Eur J Migr Law 16(1):69–95

Chapter 2
The EU and the Ineffectiveness of Expulsion Policies

The European Migration Agenda, adopted by the European Commission in May 2015, acknowledged that the EU expulsions system is "ineffective" in view of the rates of successful returns of third-country nationals given a removal order. In order to tackle this challenge, the Agenda called for ensuring that third countries fulfil their international obligation to take back their own nationals residing irregularly in Europe, particularly in the context of readmission instruments.[1]

In a letter drafted by the European Commissioner for Migration, Home Affairs and Citizenship Dimitris Avramopoulos to EU Member States on 9 June 2015 a similar issue was raised. The letter stated that "one of the incentives for irregular migration is the knowledge that the EU's system to return irregular migrants, or those whose asylum applications are rejected, is not sufficiently fast and effective".[2] The Commissioner highlighted that "we must make sure that the countries of origin of these irregular migrants cooperate and take them back." The letter expressed concerns about EU Member States' lack of enforcement of removal orders and the "low rate of returns"—less than 40 % during 2014—which in his view jeopardized the credibility of EU policy seeking to reduce irregular immigration.[3] The annex of the letter included a Paper titled "Increasing the effectiveness of the EU system to return irregular migrants" which offered a number of concrete policy measures aimed at making return effective; i.e. increasing the rates of return. The paper first calls for the need to better enforce return by focusing on the "immediate identification of migrants upon arrival" and obtaining the necessary travel documents for readmission.

The paper referred to the role by Frontex (the EU external borders agency) in providing assistance to EU Member States in identification under the Hotspot

---

[1] European Commission (2015a), p. 9.
[2] Council of the EU (2015b).
[3] Ibid. The letter stated that "Statistical data show that certain Member States are more effective than others in returning irregular migrants (the return rates of EU Member States range between 15 and 95 %, according to Eurostat data). Some enjoy better practical cooperation with certain countries of origin than others. Best practices in overcoming obstacles to efficient returns in national laws, regulations and administrative practices should be systematically identified and shared", p. 3.

approach in Greece and Italy[4] and "obtaining the documents for readmission by taking the necessary steps with the authorities of the countries of origin, on behalf of EU Member States". The Hotspot model entails the deployment of operational support by EU agencies such as Frontex, but also Europol and European Asylum Support Office (EASO), involved in the screening of TCNs (identification, fingerprinting and registration), provision of information and assistance to applicants of international protection and the preparation and removal of irregular immigrants.[5] Following identification, the paper added, "Member States should use more systematically the possibility to return irregular migrants through Joint Return Operations organized and/or coordinated by Frontex".

The Commission has more recently reported that "Frontex [guest officers] will support the Greek authorities in verifying the identity of third country nationals and whether they have been registered in the relevant databases" in Greece.[6] It recommended that "IT systems should be updated to first deploy a fully-fledged Automated Fingerprinting Identification System (AFIS) and then to ensure that interconnections between national and EU/international databases are established, thereby allowing for a full check of arriving migrants against Schengen Information System (SIS) II/Interpol Stolen and Lost Travel Documents (STLD) databases." Similar recommendations were advanced for the Hotspots in Italy.[7]

Increasing return rates were also confirmed as a priority by the Commission's "EU Action Plan on Return" of September 2015 and as the most important way of enhancing the efficiency of the EU expulsion system.[8] The Commission emphasized that boosting cooperation in returns and readmission with main countries of origin and transit of irregular immigrants constituted an essential ingredient for increasing the return rates. The Action Plan also underlined that expulsion is easier with countries that have entered into an EURA with the EU.

The Council Conclusions on the future of the returns policy adopted by EU Member States' representatives in October 2015 welcomed the Commission's calls for increasing the capacity of the Member States to return irregular migrants.[9] Member States sent 'the ball back' to the EU authorities by stating that both "The EU and its Member States must do more in terms of return."[10] The Conclusions insisted on what has become a mantra in recent decades of European cooperation on migration with third countries: the European Commission should ensure that "ongoing negotiations on readmission agreements are accelerated and concluded as soon as possible."[11] In this context, the Council welcomed the further development

---

[4]European Commission (2015b).
[5]Carrera and Guild (2015), Guild et al. (2015).
[6]European Commission (2016b).
[7]European Commission (2016c).
[8]European Commission (2015c).
[9]Council of the EU (2015a), Council of the EU (2015b).
[10]Idid. Paragraph 5.
[11]Ibid. Paragraph 11.

of the 'more for more' principle (conditionality) as a way to increase the Commission's leverage when attempting to persuade third countries to sign EURAs.[12]

The Conclusions also invited the European Commission and the European External Action Service (EEAS) to promote the EU *laissez-passer* (standard document for expulsion of TCNs) in order for it to become the commonly accepted travel document for expulsion procedures.[13] The European Commission presented a proposal for a European travel document for the return of illegally staying TCNs on 15 December 2015.[14] The proposal underlines that "the effective return of third country nationals who do not fulfil or no longer fulfil the conditions for entry, stay or residence …is an essential part of a comprehensive approach to ensure the proper functioning of the EU migration policies and for maintaining public trust in the Union migration system".[15] The proposal for a Regulation also emphasizes that the lack of valid travel documents issued by the country of destination of the person to be removed constitutes one of the most important obstacles to 'successful return'. It concluded that the recognition of the 1994 EU standard travel document is low "because of its unsatisfactory security features and standards".[16] The proposal, which is currently under inter-institutional negotiations, would introduce a new common format for a European travel document for return aimed at ensuring "high technical and security standards".[17]

---

[12]In paragraph 12 emphasizes that "The Council welcomes the introduction of the more-for-more principle as a way to increase the EU's and Member States' leverage. A fine balance of incentives and pressure should be used to enhance the cooperation of third-countries on readmission and return. This principle must therefore be applied more broadly and actively used in a concerted way, at both EU and national level, linking improved cooperation on return and readmission to benefits in all policy areas, building on the experience with the pilot projects on return. The Council calls on the Commission, together with the EEAS, to propose, within six months, comprehensive and tailor-made packages to be used vis-à-vis third-countries in order to remedy problems encountered in implementing effective readmission. Such packages should be implemented immediately afterwards. Conditionality should be used where appropriate with the aim to improving cooperation. In this context, Member States are encouraged to identify leverage in the areas that fall under their national competence."

[13]Council of the EU (1994).

[14]European Commission (2015d).

[15]Ibid, p. 2.

[16]The proposal states that "The objective of this proposal is to establish a dedicated European travel document for the return of third-country nationals subject to a return decision, which provides for a uniform format and enhanced technical and security features to ensure a wider acceptance by third countries and the increased use of such document for the purpose of readmission. Its use should be promoted in EU and bilateral readmission or other agreements", p. 2.

[17]Paragraph 11 of the Preface states that "The Content and technical specifications of the European travel document for return should be harmonized in order to ensure high technical and security standards, in particular as regards safeguards against counterfeiting and falsification. The document should be recognizable harmonized security features. High technical and security standards already exist and are set according to Article 2 of the Council Regulation No. 333/2002, which should therefore be applied to the European travel document for return". Refer to Article 4 of the proposal.

Another recent priority has given preference to informal or legally non-binding EU working arrangements on readmission in the scope of so-called high-level migration dialogues of the EU. This working logic is evident in the Action Plan agreed by EU Member States in the Valletta Summit of 11 and 12 November 2015 which concluded the priority to "develop practical cooperation arrangements and bilateral dialogues on implementation of returns with regard, in particular, to identification and issuance of travel documents".[18] A first outcome has been the Joint Declaration on Ghana-EU Cooperation on Migration of 16 April 2016, which states in paragraph 11 that "… both parties agreed on the need to significantly increase in the short-term the speed and efficiency of procedures for returning and receiving irregular migrants and the timely issuance of travel documents required for return. The parties agreed to deepen the discussions at the technical level. Ghanaian authorities committed to organize pilot identification missions in EU Member States [not later than June 2016]".[19]

One of the most visible priorities of the EU responses to the 2015–2016 'European refugee crisis' has been facilitating the identification of TCNs for the purposes of expulsion. The Commission Communication "Towards a reform of the common European asylum system and enhancing legal avenues to Europe" COM (2016) 197 of 6 April 2016 called Member States of first entry in Schengen territory to "identify, register, and fingerprint all migrants, and return those not in need of protection." The Communication advanced a legislative reform of the large-scale database Eurodac, which currently includes data and biometrics of asylum seekers in the EU.[20] Controversially, the Commission announced the plan to

> …extend the scope of Eurodac as a means to contribute to the fight against irregular migration by allowing the system to be used to facilitate the return of irregular migrants. In doing so, Eurodac will be used as a means to accelerate the identification and re-documentation of migrants and will enable a better assessment of the prospect of absconding, thus enhancing the effectiveness and speed of return and readmission procedures.[21]

---

[18]Valletta Summit (2015). See also paragraph 9 of the Valletta Summit Political Declaration, which states that "We are determined to strengthen the fight against irregular migration in line with existing agreements and obligations under international law, as well as mutually agreed arrangements on return and readmission. We agree to give preference to voluntary return and reaffirm that all returns must be carried out in full respect of human rights and human dignity. We will improve cooperation on return and sustainable reintegration which can only enhance migration and mobility policy and make it more effective and comprehensive."

[19]The Joint Declaration states in paragraph 11 that: "Both parties agreed that an effective return policy is an integral part of migration management and will deter further irregular migration. The National Migration Policy for Ghana identifies return, readmission and reintegration of emigrant Ghanaians and recognizes the challenges in this area". See http://eeas.europa.eu/statements-eeas/2016/160416_04_en.htm.

[20]European Commission (2016d).

[21]The Communication stipulates that "expanding the purpose of Eurodac beyond asylum is relevant considering Member States' difficulties to effectively monitor the irregular entries at the external borders and subsequent movements. Eurodac can be used to substantially enhance

The Council Conclusions "on the expulsion of illegally present third country nationals" adopted in May 2016 emphasized that the previously mentioned legally non-binding EU readmission informal arrangements should pertain in particular own nationals.[22] In the same vein, the Council Conclusions "External aspects of migration" of 23 May 2016 called for the full implementation of the Valletta Action Plan and the need "for full and effective implementation of existing readmission agreements" as central components of "the external aspects of the European Agenda on Migration".[23] The Conclusions highlighted: "the Council, in close cooperation with the Commission, is committed to enhanced and more effective cooperation on return with key countries of origins and transit, in particular with Pakistan, Afghanistan and Bangladesh".

The Commission Communication "on establishing a new Partnership Framework with third countries under the European Migration Agenda" of 7 June 2016 re-stated the need to increase returns rates to countries of origin and transit as a part of a "new comprehensive cooperation with third countries on migration".[24] The Commission expressed its plans to develop "comprehensive partnerships (compacts) with third countries", which would chiefly aim at including joint efforts to make readmission and return work. The Communication underlined the need to ensure that third countries readmit their nationals by focusing on:

> Coordinated and coherent EU and Member State coordination on readmission where the paramount priority is to achieve fast and operational returns, and not necessarily formal readmission agreements. The facilitation of the identification of irregular migrants in view of their readmission by strengthening third countries' capacity to ensure functioning civil registries and fingerprint or biometrics digitalisation, as well as capacity building on border and migration management. Stepping up Assisted Voluntary Return and Reintegration initiatives on the route to help countries of transit in returning third country nationals to their countries of origin whenever possible, including promoting regional cooperation among countries of origin and transit. The acceptance by partner countries to use the EU laissez-passer for return operations.

(Footnote 21 continued)

Member States' ability to track irregular migrants in the EU by storing fingerprint data under all categories and allowing comparisons to be made with all stored data", p. 9.

[22]Council of the EU (2016b).

[23]Council of the EU (2016a), para. 8. The Council also welcomed "The Commission's recommendation to authorize the opening of negotiations on a readmission agreement between the EU and the Republic of Nigeria". Ibid. Paragraph 9 of the Conclusions state: "The combination of dialogues, missions and instruments outlined above must lead to visible improvement in the cooperation with key partner countries. This approach, as part of a strategic and operational plan, based on concrete short, medium and long-term measures, should be a central part of the external aspects of the European Agenda on Migration and the further preparations of the June European Council".

[24]European Commission (2016a), p. 7. As part of the "long-term objectives" the Communication stated that "As regards Asia, Afghanistan is a major source of irregular migrants and of refugees arriving to Europe. While continuing its long-standing effort to support the stabilisation of the country, the EU should step up its engagement to ensure Afghanistan's cooperation on readmission. Other priority countries of origin in Asia are Pakistan and Bangladesh", p. 16.

Open Access This chapter is distributed under the terms of the Creative Commons Attribution 4.0 International License (http://creativecommons.org/licenses/by/4.0/), which permits use, duplication, adaptation, distribution and reproduction in any medium or format, as long as you give appropriate credit to the original author(s) and the source, a link is provided to the Creative Commons license and any changes made are indicated.

The images or other third party material in this chapter are included in the work's Creative Commons license, unless indicated otherwise in the credit line; if such material is not included in the work's Creative Commons license and the respective action is not permitted by statutory regulation, users will need to obtain permission from the license holder to duplicate, adapt or reproduce the material.

References

Carrera S, Guild E (2015) Can the new refugee relocation system work? Perils in the Dublin logic and flawed reception conditions in the EU. CEPS Policy Brief, Brussels
Council of the EU (1994) Recommendation of 30 November 1994 concerning the adoption of a standard travel document for the expulsion of third-country nationals
Council of the EU (2015b) Increasing the effectiveness of the EU system to return irregular migrants. 10170/15, Brussels, 22 June 2015
Council of the EU (2016a) Conclusions on the external aspects of migration. 9111/16, Brussels, 23 May 2016
Council of the EU (2016b) Conclusions on the expulsion of illegally staying third country nationals. 8828/16, Brussels, 11 May 2016
European Commission (2015a) A European agenda on migration. COM (2015) 240, 13 May 2015
European Commission (2015b) Communication Managing the refugee crisis: State of play of the implementation of the priority actions under the European agenda on migration. COM (2015) 510, 14 November 2015
European Commission (2015c) EU action plan on return. COM (2015) 453, 9 September 2015
European Commission (2015d) Proposal for a Regulation on a European travel document for the return of illegally staying third country nationals. COM (2015) 668, 15 December 2015
European Commission (2016a) on establishing a new Partnership Framework with third countries under the European Migration Agenda, COM (2016) 385, 7 July 2016
European Commission (2016b) Annex to the Commission Communication on the state of play of implementation of the priority actions under the European agenda on migration: Greece - State of play report, COM (2016) 85, 10 Feb 2016
European Commission (2016c) Annex to the Commission Communication on the state of play of implementation of the priority actions under the European agenda on migration: Italy - state of play report, COM (2016) 85, 10 Feb 2016
European Commission (2016d) Proposal for a Regulation on the establishment of 'Eurodac' for the comparison of fingerprints for the effective application of [Regulation (EU) No 604/2013 establishing the criteria and mechanisms for determining the Member State responsible for examining an application for international protection lodged in one of the Member States by a third-country national or a stateless person], for identifying an illegally staying third-country national or stateless person and on requests for the comparison with Eurodac data by Member States' law enforcement authorities and Europol for law enforcement purposes (recast). COM (2016) 272 final, 4 May 2016
Guild E, Costello C, Garlick M, Moreno-Lax V (2015) Enhancing the common European asylum system and alternatives to Dublin. CEPS Paper in Liberty and Security in Europe, Brussels
Valletta Summit (2015) Action Plan 11/12 Nov 2015

Chapter 3
Identity Determination Dilemmas: Whose National Are You?

The European Commission and EU Member States make often reference to the unwillingness of third countries to readmit their own nationals as one of the main obstacles for increasing return rates. The scholarly debate has identified the main obstacles facing the negotiations and operability of EURAs. EURAs present a high level of dependency on the state of diplomatic relations between the states concerned. The academic literature has illustrated the importance of the role and cooperation of third country consular authorities in the workability or concrete implementation of readmission procedures, and the development of formal and informal patterns of cooperation covering 'readmission' which has been based on administrative arrangements, bilateral deals and exchanges of letters/memoranda of understanding as complementary to RAs.[1]

In its evaluation of EURAs in 2011 the European Commission underlined the policy inconsistency resulting from certain EU Member States still their bilateral arrangements that pre-dated the EURA.[2] This has been a key point of discussion in the lifespan of EURAs during the last three decades.[3] Suffice it to say that as instruments aimed at shaping international or inter-state relations in migration management, RAs depend on the state of diplomatic relations with the third (non-EU) country concerned. This dependency factor unlocks a series of practical challenges related to inter-state diplomacy and in handling conflicting sovereign interests at stake in expulsion procedures.

Cassarino has argued that "while incentives play a crucial role in inducing third countries to cooperate on readmission, they do not adequately account for the sustainability of bilateral cooperation in the long term". In his view this is mainly

---

[1]Cassarino (2010).
[2]European Commission (2011). The Commission stated "The reasons given for non-application of EURAs are the absence of a bilateral implementing protocol and/or that EURAs are used only if they facilitate returns. Whereas transition periods for third country nationals in certain EURAs as well as the need to adapt national administrative procedures may explain the continued use of bilateral agreements in certain cases, the absence of implementing protocols8 is not an excuse.", p. 4.
[3]Panizon (2012), Coleman (2009).

due to the "asymmetrical impact of the effective implementation of the agreements".[4] Requested states do not often deliver the necessary travel documents or do not reply (on time or at all) to EU Member States' readmission requests. Cassarino refers to the pressing challenge of re-documentation (i.e. "the delivery of travel documents or *laissez-passers* by the consular authorities of the third country needed to remove irregular migrants") as an area where informal and bilateral (readmission deals) between EU Member States and third countries have progressively developed.[5] The issue of re-documentation and lack of cooperation of third countries to readmit individuals identified as their own nationals, however, hides a more profound and far-reaching dilemma that is inherent to the practical implementation of the readmission logic and which has not received much detailed attention in the academic debate.

A field where asymmetries emerge in the readmission field relate to identifying who is a national of which state. The implementation of expulsion faces a deeper disagreement between the states concerned as to whether the person(s) involved are indeed nationals of the assigned or presumed country of origin. As noted in Chap. 2 above, when measuring effectiveness, the European Commission puts particular emphasis on the low rates of expulsions and why removal orders are not enforced by EU Member State authorities. The above-mentioned letter issued by European Commissioner Avramopoulos declared that one of the main reasons why removal orders are not enforced relate to a "lack of cooperation from the individuals concerned (they conceal their identity or abscond) or from their countries of origin (for instance problems in obtaining the necessary documentation from consular authorities)".[6]

The difficulties in determining legal identity has been also highlighted in studies and Ad Hoc Queries issued by the European Migration Network (EMN). An EMN Ad Hoc Query on EU Laissez-Passer of October 2010 covered the obstacles experienced by some EU Member States in the processes of identification of the person to be readmitted, in particular when it comes to travelling documentation. The Query highlighted that often third countries are unwilling to cooperate with requesting EU states in the process of identifying the nationality of the person involved "because in many cases they have little or no interest in readmitting their own nationals". According to countries like Germany, as the issuing of an EU *Laissez-Passer* ultimately requires the identification of a person's nationality, modifying it would do little to address this fundamental issue. In the same vein, Sweden reported that "Even if the document quality would be improved, we would still have problems when it comes to the available information about the holder's identity."

In a 2012 report titled "Practical Measures to reduce irregular immigration" and funded by the European Commission, the EMN pointed out a number of situations where expulsions prove problematic. These included (i) a lack of cooperation of the

---

[4]Cassarino (2007), p. 192.
[5]Ibid. p. 187.
[6]Council of the EU (2015).

country of origin and their unwillingness to readmit their own citizens; (ii) difficulties in establishing a person's identity and the lack of travel documents; and (iii) an unwillingness on the part of individuals to cooperate in their own removal.[7] Similar issues were identified in another EMN study from 2013 titled "Establishing Identity for International Protection: Challenges and Practices".[8] The EMN examined the ways in which EU Member States understand the concept of 'identity' within expulsion procedures. A majority of EU States reported that "In the absence of valid proof of identity, the authorities responsible for executing returns have to request travel documents for the applicant from his/her (declared) country of origin. Cooperation with third countries, including in the context of readmission agreements, affects success in this regard".[9] Another finding was that the type of documents accepted by countries of origin varies widely, depending on the type of expulsion procedures.[10]

The 2013 EMN study illustrates how contacts with the national authorities of the 'presumed' country of origin were reported to be *indispensable* in expulsion procedures, and that there were strict demands for documenting identity in these cases, sometimes including coercive methods.[11] The annex of the EMN study lays down a compilation of methods used by EU national authorities in determining the identity of the persons to be expelled. While citizenship constitutes the most important element in determining legal status, the study presents other methods used by relevant national authorities in EU Member States such as language analysis, age assessment, comparison of fingerprints and photographs with national or EU databases, DNA analysis, interviews, consultations with country liaison officers based in the (presumed) countries of origin, coercive methods (including forced searches of the applicant's property), biometrics, etc.[12] According to the study,

> In the domain of 'forced return', the identity question is often decisive regarding the possibility for return. To implement a 'forced return', the identity of the person concerned must either be verified (by the country of return) or documented (with valid passport or travel document) in a way accepted by the perceived country of origin.[13]

All these challenges remain despite the fact that a subsequent EMN published in 2014 stated that statistics provided by some EU Member States indicated that the

---

[7]EMN (2012).
[8]EMN (2013).
[9]Ibid. p. 7.
[10]Ibid. p. 15.
[11]Ibid.
[12]Table 7 in the Annex of EMN (2013). See Table 5 on the kind of documents accepted.
[13]Ibid. p. 22. The Study emphasizes that "The presence of reliable identity and travel documents is often decisive, as most countries of origin request a person identified by nationality, surname, first name and date of birth. Exceptionally, determining the nationality of the rejected applicant may suffice to launch the return process. In Greece, for example, return may take place even with partial identity even though personal data about the applicant has not been absolutely verified. On the other hand, in Italy, identification does not affect the decision on forced return, as this procedure may be started only with an attribution of identity".

majority (almost 100 %) of applications lodged by Member States covered own nationals of the countries with whom EURAs have been concluded.[14] Identification challenges have been also reported in monitoring reporting procedures of removal regimes such as the one in the UK. Another report published in 2015 by the UK Independent Chief Inspector of Borders and Immigration highlighted: "We were told by the Home Office that there are some countries to where removal cannot be enforced, either because of the general situation prevailing in that country or because of an unwillingness on the part of the country to document its own nationals, e.g. Iran".[15] It is therefore clear that a third-country national cannot be readmitted when her/his identity is not adequately established. Two specific examples illustrate ongoing frictions related to the identity determination challenge: First, the obstacles in the implementation of the EURA with Pakistan (Sect. 3.1), and second, the UK Supreme Court judgment in *Pham v. Secretary of State for the Home Department* (Sect. 3.2 below).

3.1 The Quasi-suspension of the EURA with Pakistan

A recent controversy in the application of the EURA with Pakistan illustrates some of the previously identified dilemmas in the operability of readmission. The unclear situation of 'Afghan nationals from Pakistan' constituted an issue of concern from the very start of EU talks on migration and asylum with Pakistan in the late 1990s.[16] The EURA with Pakistan entered into force in 2010.[17] Five years later, and in the context of the so-called European refugee crisis, the Pakistani authorities reportedly

---

[14]EMN (2014).

[15]Independent Chief Inspector of Borders and Immigration (2015).

[16]Council of the EU (1999). The Action Plan for Afghanistan states in paragraph 54 that "At present, about 1, 2 million Afghan nationals live as refugees in Pakistan (the total number is, however, estimated at 2 million). In comparison with 1989, when the number of Afghan refugees exceeded 3 million, this is a strong decrease. Especially since 1992, after the fall of the Najibullah regime, the repatriation of Afghan nationals gained momentum. During the last few years, the number of Afghans returning to their country has however decreased. Nevertheless, in 1998 UNHCR repatriated 93,200 Afghan nationals from Pakistan. As always with UNHCR, these people returned voluntarily." Moreover, paragraph 62 emphasized that "A declaration is appended to the EC-Pakistan Co-operation Agreement in which Pakistan declares its willingness to conclude readmission agreements with the Member States which so request. The agreement is due to be signed in [....] 1999. Since the declaration refers only to the readmission of "nationals" (viz. Pakistani), the declaration does not explicitly include the readmission of Afghans who have arrived in the EU via Pakistan. At present, Pakistan does not appear to be officially prepared to readmit Afghans who have been resident for a long period in an EU Member State. According to the Pakistani authorities, the Afghan refugee problem has simply internationalised with tens of thousands seeking asylum in Western Europe while Pakistan still harbors a multiple of that number. The fact that a number of Afghans hold Pakistani travel documents makes little difference, as the great majority of such documents are thought to have been obtained illegally, according to the Pakistani authorities."

[17]OJ L 287/52 4 November 2010.

announced in November 2015 the unilateral suspension in the application of the EURA because it argued that some deportations were unfounded.[18] A representative from the Interior Ministry of Pakistan declared that readmissions had taken place "without proper determination they were Pakistan nationals".[19] The Minister of Interior also announced that "Pakistan would not accept any deportees accused of militant [terrorism] links without clear evidence of guilt". A joint return flight coordinated by Frontex from Greece on 4 November 2015 was not permitted to disembark 70 persons to be readmitted as Pakistani nationals.[20]

The Commission's Communication on "Managing the refugee crisis: State of Play of the Implementation of the Priority Actions under the European Agenda on Migration" COM (2015) 510 of November 2015 emphasised: "A particular blockage was identified in Greece, resulting from disputes concerning documentation".[21] The Communication specified that "dedicated readmission discussions between the Commission, Greece and the Pakistani authorities" should lead to "a joint understanding on the application of the EU readmission agreement between Greece and Pakistan". According to interviews conducted for the purposes of this book with EU policy makers in Brussels, even if the person to be readmitted has a passport issued by Pakistan, Pakistani authorities don't seem to accept the readmission request if the passport does not have biometric identifiers and the name of the person is included in their national biometric database.[22] These same interviews raised concerns about the non-reliability and "untrustworthiness" of the Pakistani biometric system at times of establishing the legal identity of the person involved.

On 23 November 2015 Commissioner Avramopoulos visited Pakistan to discuss and agree a way forward in the situation. After the meeting Avramopoulos declared that "everything is back to normal" and that "the EU would work with Pakistan to improve its verifications of citizenship before sending anyone back to Pakistan".[23] In a meeting of the Civil Liberties, Justice and Home Affairs (LIBE) Committee of the European Parliament on 16 February 2016, the European Commission DG Home Affairs updated MEPs on the state of affairs with all EURAs. The Commission stated that a meeting had taken place on the 2 February 2016 with the Pakistani authorities in the context of the Joint Readmission Committee and that "concrete steps" were agreed to steer the implementation of the agreement. In particular, the Commission clarified that the Joint Readmission Committee had

---

[18]Refer to The Express Tribune (2015). The spokesperson on Pakistan Ministry of Interior declared that "The signing country had to first verify the nationality of that person who was being deported but there were instances where the nationality was not being verified. The minister took notice and the agreement is temporarily suspended." See Dawn (2015a, b).
[19]Ibid.
[20]Frontex (2015).
[21]European Commission (2015).
[22]It appears that Pakistan is considering setting up another database exclusively for the purposes of readmission and that the country plans to start issuing only biometric passports before the end of 2016.
[23]Reuters (2015).

agreed operational arrangements with Pakistan, including a number of concrete actions to deal with current obstacles.

The operational arrangements agreed with Pakistan remain confidential. The Commission's intervention before the EP LIBE Committee highlighted that they include a plan to organise a joint identification mission, which appears to be still in the planning stage. This would bring Pakistani authorities to Greece and jointly participate in the identification procedures, particularly in those cases where the identity is disputed, as well as in fostering the use of biometric technologies in the processing of readmission. The operational arrangements also foresee the obligation by Pakistani authorities to reply on specific deadlines for readmission requests by EU Member States. There continue to be obstacles when 'readmitting' people from Greece to Pakistan. According to interviews, Pakistani authorities continue not to reply within the stipulated deadlines. As of May 2016, Greece has reported a backlog of 592 readmission requests unanswered by the Pakistani authorities. This picture corresponds with the situation described by a study published by the European Migration Network (EMN) in 2014, which stated:

> ...the EURA with Pakistan is assessed as problematic due to delays in response and various other practical obstacles, such as the loss of documents. The average response time also reflects the disparity in the effectiveness between EURAs concluded with different third countries. For example, while the average response time for Georgia is 6-7 days, in the exceptional case of the EURA with Pakistan, it can take over a year to obtain a response from the authorities.[24]

It is no clear at the time of writing how the obstacles in the EURA with Pakistan will be overcome. A Frontex Evaluation Report, issued 2 December 2015 on a Joint Return Operation from Greece to Pakistan,[25] identified ongoing identification issues when stating that

> Only 19 returnees (13 from Greece, 4 from Austria and 2 from Bulgaria) were successfully handed over in Islamabad. Despite the fact that also the other 30 returnees (26 from Greece, 2 from Austria and 2 from Bulgaria) were holding valid passports and/or travel documents, they were not authorize to disembark the aircraft as, according to new rules imposed by the Pakistani authorities, their identity had not been "verified" prior to the flight by their Ministry of the Interior through supplementary biometric checks. Those 30 Pakistani citizens were brought back to Athens on board the same charter flight.

---

[24]EMN (2014) p. 22.

[25]Frontex (2015). The Report states that "As a result of a visit to the Embassy of Pakistan in Athens of a delegation headed by the European Commission aimed at increasing the commitment of the Pakistani authorities towards the identification of their nationals expelled from Greece awaiting to be returned in local detention centres, at the end of October the Greek authorities succeed in obtaining travel documents for around 70 Pakistani citizens. Frontex invited Greece to organize as soon as possible a joint return operation by air to Pakistan which was planned on the 4.11.2015. Due to the temporarily unavailability of the Greek authorities to hire planes, Frontex requested the cooperation of other MS and obtained the availability of Denmark to charter a suitable aircraft." Information on all Joint Return Operations can be found here: http://frontex.europa.eu/operations/archive-of-operations/?year=2015&type=Return&host Accessed on 31 May 2016.

3.2 Pham v. Secretary of State for the Home Department Case

The 2015 *Pham* Case provides another example of inter-state challenges inherent to the 'readmission logic'. The UK Supreme Court issued on the 25 March 2015 the judgment on the case.[26] The case related to the lawfulness of the UK Home Department's decision to deprive the appellant of his British citizenship as it would render him stateless. The main point of contestation was the extent to which the UK authorities should take account before depriving the appellant of British nationality of the fact that according to Vietnamese authorities he was not a national of Vietnam "under the operation of its law" in light of Article 1.1 of the 1954 Convention relating to the Status of Stateless Persons.[27]

The appellant was born in Vietnam in 1983 and hence acquired Vietnamese nationality. The family went to the UK in 1989, claimed asylum and were granted indefinite leave to remain in the country. Six years later they acquired British citizenship. Between end of 2010 and summer 2011 the appellant was in Yemen where "according to UK security services but denied by him, he is said to have received terrorist training from Al Qaeda. It is the assessment of the security services that at liberty he would pose an active threat to the safety and security of this country". On the basis of his suspected involvement in terrorist activities he was deprived of British nationality. Ever since Vietnamese authorities have declined to recognise him as a national of Vietnam.

Mr. Pham appealed this decision before the Special Immigration Appeals Commission (SIAC), on various grounds, including the one that the decision would render him stateless as well as the compatibility of the decision in light of EU citizenship law. The Court of Appeals held that Mr. Pham was a Vietnamese national on the relevant date under Vietnamese nationality laws. The Court concluded:

> If the Government of the foreign state chooses to act contrary to its own law, it may render the individual de facto stateless. Our own courts, however, must respect the rule of law and cannot characterise the individual as de jure stateless. If this outcome is regarded as unsatisfactory, the remedy is to expand the definition of stateless persons in the 1954 Convention or in the 1981 Act, as some have urged. The remedy is not to subvert the rule of law. The rule of law is now a universal concept. It is the essence of the judicial function to uphold it.[28]

The case reached the UK Supreme Court which ultimately (and unanimously) dismissed the appeal and confirmed the Court of Appeal's rejection of Mr. Pham's

---

[26]UK Supreme Court, *Pham v. Secretary of State for the Home Department* [2015] UKSC 19, On appeal from [2013] EWCA Civ 616.
[27]4 UNTS 360, 130.
[28]Paragraph 92 of the judgment of the Court of Appeal.

claim and validated the decision by the UK Secretary of State for the Home Department. The Supreme Court held that there was no evidence "of a decision or practice of the Vietnam government which treated the appellant as a non-national "by operation of its law" or a decision effective at the date of the Home Secretary's decision of 22 December 2011.[29] The Supreme Court also covered the compatibility of the decision with EU citizenship law and case-law by the Court of Justice of the European Union (CJEU), which is examined in detail in Sect. 5.3 of this book below. The UK Supreme Court reached the opinion that it was not necessary to resolve the dispute in light of EU law, and in particular the EU general principle of proportionality. It concluded in this regard that:

> The issue would need to be considered by the domestic courts before it would be appropriate to consider a reference to the CJEU. However, before that stage is reached it is important that the tribunal of fact, SIAC, should first identify the respects in which a decision on these legal issues might be necessary for disposal of the case, including how the EU requirement of proportionality would differ in practice in the present case from proportionality under the European Convention on Human Rights, an issue already before SIAC, or from applying domestic law principles.[30]

Open Access This chapter is distributed under the terms of the Creative Commons Attribution 4.0 International License (http://creativecommons.org/licenses/by/4.0/), which permits use, duplication, adaptation, distribution and reproduction in any medium or format, as long as you give appropriate credit to the original author(s) and the source, a link is provided to the Creative Commons license and any changes made are indicated.

The images or other third party material in this chapter are included in the work's Creative Commons license, unless indicated otherwise in the credit line; if such material is not included in the work's Creative Commons license and the respective action is not permitted by statutory regulation, users will need to obtain permission from the license holder to duplicate, adapt or reproduce the material.

---

[29] Refer to paragraphs 34–38 of the judgement.

[30] See paragraphs 58 and 59 of the ruling. Paragraph 71 of the judgment held that "For reasons which will appear, I consider that it is unnecessary and inappropriate at least at this stage to resolve the disagreement between the parties about Union law, or to consider making any reference to the Court of Justice relating to it. The right course is to remit the matter to SIAC, with an indication that it should address the issues in the case on alternative hypotheses, one that the Court of Appeal's decision in R (G1) v. Secretary of State is correct, the other that it is incorrect." Furthermore in paragraph 98 the Court considered that the principle of 'reasonableness' and the EU proportionality principle were of a similar legal nature: "If and so far as a withdrawal of nationality by the United Kingdom would at the same time mean loss of European citizenship, that is an additional detriment which a United Kingdom court could also take into account, when considering whether the withdrawal was under United Kingdom law proportionate. It is therefore improbable that the nature, strictness or outcome of such a review would differ according to whether it was conducted under domestic principles or whether it was also required to be conducted by reference to a principle of proportionality derived from Union law".

References

Cassarino JP (2007) Informalising readmission agreements in the EU neighbourhood. Int Spectator 42(2):179–196

Cassarino JP (ed) (2010) Unbalanced reciprocities: cooperation on readmission in the Euro-Mediterranean area. Special Edition Viewpoints. Middle East Institute, Washington

Coleman N (2009) European readmission policy. Third country interests and refugee rights. Martinus Nijhoff, Leiden

Council of the EU (1999) Action plan for Afghanistan. 11424/99, Brussels, 30 Sep 1999

Council of the EU (2015) Increasing the effectiveness of the EU system to return irregular migrants. 10170/15, Brussels, 22 June 2015

Dawn (2015a) Pakistan suspends readmission agreements with Western countries, 6 November 2015. Accessed 31 May 2016

Dawn (2015b) Pakistan demands 'proof' of terror charges for deportees, 17 November 2015. Accessed 31 May 2016

European Commission (2011) Evaluation of EU readmission agreements. COM (2011) 76, 23 Feb 2011

European Commission (2015) Communication Managing the refugee crisis: State of play of the implementation of the priority actions under the European agenda on migration. COM (2015) 510, 14 Nov 2015

European Migration Network (EMN) (2012) Practical measures to reduce irregular migration. European Commission, Brussels

European Migration Network (EMN) (2013) Establishing identify for international protection: Challenges and practices. European Commission, Brussels

European Migration Network (EMN) (2014) Good practices in the return and reintegration of irregular migrants: Member states' entry bans policies and use of readmission agreements between Member States and third countries. European Commission, Brussels

Frontex (2015) Evaluation report joint return operation Greece to Pakistan. Warsaw, 2 December 2015

Independent Chief Inspector of Borders and Immigration (2015) An Inspection of Removals. London, UK, October 2014–March 2015

Panizon M (2012) Readmission agreements of EU member states: a case for EU subsidiarity or dualism? Refugee Surv Q 31(4):101–133

Reuters (2015) EU says fixes deportee deal with Pakistan after spat, 23 Nov 2015

The Express Tribune (2015) Pakistan suspends deal to accept deportations from Europe, 18 November 2015. Accessed 31 May 2016

Chapter 4
EURAs Compared

How do the EURAs deal with the identity determination dilemmas? This chapter provides a comparative assessment of the procedures and administrative rules envisaged by six EURAs as regards the identity determination of nationals to be readmitted. How do the EURAs envisage the ways in which the nationality of the person involved is to be determined and what are the main means of evidence? The EURA with Pakistan is taken as the basis of comparison with the five EURAs that have been concluded since 2011, i.e. Armenia, Azerbaijan, Cape Verde, Georgia and Turkey. EURAs aim at establishing effective and swift procedures for the identification and return of persons who do not or who no longer, fulfill the conditions for entry to, presence in, or residence on the territories of EU Member States and the third country concerned, as well as to facilitate the transit of such persons. These include own nationals of the requested state, TCNs and/or stateless persons.[1] Are there any commonalities and/or differences between the EURAs under analysis when it comes to nationality determination procedures?

The official criteria that have been used by the Council of the EU when choosing third countries with which to negotiate EURAs have mainly included the following[2]: (i) the scale of the phenomenon of irregular immigration from that country, the number of persons awaiting return and obstacles to the enforcement of repatriation decisions in particular in obtaining travel documents; (ii) the fact that the third country is geographically adjacent to a Member State; (iii) can potentially add value

---

[1] Article 1.a of the EURA with Azerbaijan (and differently from all the previous EURAs) includes a definition of 'readmission' which states that "Readmission shall mean the transfer by the Requesting State and admission by the Requested State of persons (own nationals of the Requested State, third country nationals or stateless persons) who have been found illegally entering into, present in or residing in the Requesting State, in accordance with the provision of this Agreement". A similar provision has been included in the EURA with Turkey. Refer to Article 1.n.

[2] Council of the EU (2002). The Council stated "In view of the difficulty of negotiating agreements of this kind with third countries, the countries in question need to be identified one by one, drawing upon the results of ongoing negotiations and constantly evaluating both their practical implementation and the real needs of the moment", paragraph 3.

to Member States' bilateral negotiations; (iv) countries with which the Community concluded Association and Cooperation agreements, etc. At the time of writing, the EU has concluded a total of 17 EURAs (see Table 4.1 for a detailed overview): Hong Kong (2004),[3] Macao (2004),[4] Sri Lanka (2005),[5] Albania (2006),[6] Russia (2007),[7] Macedonia (2008),[8] Ukraine (2008),[9] Moldova (2008),[10] Bosnia and Herzegovina (2008),[11] Montenegro (2008),[12] Serbia (2008),[13] Pakistan (2010),[14] Georgia (2011),[15] Armenia (2014),[16] Cape Verde (2014),[17] Azerbaijan (2014)[18] and Turkey (2014).[19]

The six EURAs under assessment start with a general article laying down key definitions. These include who is to be considered their 'nationals' for the purposes of the Agreements. The general rule is that a 'national' of the non-EU country means any person holding the nationality of that country in accordance with its legislation. This needs to be read in conjunction with the notion of 'third country national' in the scope of EURAs. In contrast to the concept normally used in EU immigration law,[20] a TCN is any person not holding the nationality of the contracting parties for the purposes of EURAs. As it will showed in this chapter and further analyzed in Chap. 5 of this book, irrespective of these two legal notions and the relevant legislation of the contracting country concerned, EURAs provide wider ways to determine an individual's identity far beyond the boundaries of nationality laws of the presumed country of origin. The EURAs laid down common procedural rules regarding the readmission obligation of own nationals (Sect. 4.1), and the general principles and means (list of documents) for establishing or presuming the nationality of the person to be readmitted (Sect. 4.2).

---

[3]OJ L 17/25 24 January 2004.
[4]OJ L 143/99 30 April 2004.
[5]OJ L 124/43 17 May 2005.
[6]OJ L 124/22 17 May 2005.
[7]OJ L 129/40 17 May 2007.
[8]OJ L 334/7 19 December 2007.
[9]OJ L 332/48 18 December 2007.
[10]OJ L 334/149 19 December 2007.
[11]OJ L 334/66 19 December 2007.
[12]OJ L 334/26 19 December 2007.
[13]OJ L 334/46 19 December 2007.
[14]OJ L 287/52 4 November 2010.
[15]OJ L 52/47 25 February 2011.
[16]OJ L 289/13 31 October 2013.
[17]OJ L 282/15 24 October 2013.
[18]OJ L 128/17 30 April 2014.
[19]OJ L 134/3 7 May 2014.
[20]In EU migration law a 'third country national' is any person not holding the nationality of an EU Member State.

Table 4.1 EURAs

Country	Mandate for negotiation	Entry into force
Morocco	September 2000	–
Sri Lanka	September 2000	1 May 2005
Pakistan	September 2000	1 December 2010
Russia	September 2000	1 June 2007
Hong Kong	April 2001	1 March 2004
Macao	April 2001	1 June 2004
Ukraine	June 2002	1 January 2008
Turkey	November 2002	1 October 2014[a]
Albania	November 2002	1 May 2006
China	November 2002	–
Algeria	November 2002	–
Macedonia	November 2006	1 January 2008
Bosnia and Herzegovina	November 2006	1 January 2008
Montenegro	November 2006	1 January 2008
Serbia	November 2006	1 January 2008
Moldova	December 2006	1 January 2008
Georgia	November 2008	1 March 2011
Cape Verde	June 2009	1 December 2014
Belarus	February 2011	–
Armenia	December 2011	1 January 2014
Azerbaijan	December 2011	1 September 2014
Tunisia	December 2014	–

[a]The EURA with Turkey entered into force on that date with the exception of Articles 4 and 6 covering third country nationals and stateless. Refer to Article 24.3 of the Agreement
Source Author's own elaboration

4.1 Readmission Obligation of Own Nationals

Section 1 of the EURAs contains the so-called readmission obligations, which include the rules applicable to the readmission of nationals, TCNs and stateless persons. It is important to first clarity that the identity determination of nationals is of crucial importance for those countries that are not geographically adjacent to EU Member States. This relates to the EURAs provisions on TCNs which increase the burden of proof by the requesting state in comparison to the readmission of own nationals. The obligation to readmit TCNs and stateless persons is conditional upon proof by the requesting state of direct and irregular entry by the person concerned into its territory after having stayed or transited through the territory of the requested state.[21] This makes the readmission of TCNs and stateless persons to countries like Pakistan almost impossible in practice.

When it comes to own nationals, Article 2 of the EURA with Pakistan states that the Requested State shall readmit "after the nationality having been proved" any of its nationals who do not or no longer fulfil the conditions for entry, presence or residence in the territory of the requesting State. A similar provision exists in the EURAs with Armenia, Azerbaijan, Cape Verde, Georgia and Turkey (see Annex of this book for a detailed overview). Yet, this same provision has been further developed and complemented in the five subsequent EURAs. The EURA with Georgia lays down in Article 2 that the obligation to readmit 'nationals' shall take place upon application by the requesting State and "without further formalities other than those provided for in this Agreement" and "provided that it is proved, or may be validly assumed on the basis of prima facie evidence furnished, that they are nationals of Georgia".

Furthermore, in contrast to the agreement with Pakistan, the EURA with Georgia also includes specific provisions within the scope of Article 2 about the obligation by Georgia to readmit the minor unmarried children as well as spouses holding another nationality of the national involved (see Article 2.2 EURA with Georgia). Similar provisions are foreseen in the subsequent EURAs with Armenia, Azerbaijan, Cape Verde, Georgia and Turkey. Sometimes these include minor modifications to the provision included in the EURA with Georgia. For instance, the EURA with Armenia includes the obligation to readmit the spouses of Armenian nationals who hold another nationality "or who are stateless". The subsequent EURAs with Cape Verde[22] and Azerbaijan also cover spouses who are stateless. This is not the case in the EURA with Turkey.

Unlike the EURA with Pakistan, the other five EURAs include a provision laying down the obligation for the requested state to readmit persons who have renounced

---

[21] For instance Article 3 (Readmission of Third Country Nationals and Stateless) of the EURA with Pakistan states that "1. The Requested State shall readmit, upon application by the Requesting State and without further formalities other than those provided for in this Agreement, any third country national or Stateless person who does not, or who no longer, fulfils the conditions in force for entry into, presence in, or residence on, the territory of the requesting State, provided that such persons: (a) hold, at the time of submission of the readmission application, a valid visa or residence authorisation issued by the Requested State; or (b) entered the territory of the Requesting State unlawfully coming directly from the territory of the Requested State. A person comes directly from the territory of the Requested State within the meaning of this subparagraph if he or she arrived on the territory of the Requesting State, or, where the Requested State is Pakistan, on the territory of the Member States, by air or ship without having entered another country in-between." See also Article 7 of the agreement which provides the means of evidence regarding third country nationals and stateless, and Annex III which stipulates the common list of documents which shall be considered as means of evidence of the conditions for the readmission of third country nationals and stateless persons (Article 3.1 in conjunction with Article 7.1).

[22] The inclusion of spouses who are stateless The EURA with Cape Verde refers in Article 2 to Article 13.5.c.i of the Cotonou Agreement. See Article 2 of EURA with Cape Verde.

4.1 Readmission Obligation of Own Nationals

or been deprived of the nationality of the non-EU country since entering the territory of an EU Member State. The Agreements state that this obligation exists "unless such persons have at least been promised naturalization by that Member State."[23] Few variations still exist. The EURA with Georgia makes reference to the need to readmit not only persons who have renounced or been deprived of Georgian nationality, but also those who have forfeited the nationality of Georgia. The EURAs with Armenia, Cape Verde and Azerbaijan only make reference to cases of renunciation of nationality, not cases of deprivation or forfeit. The EURA with Turkey includes situations of renunciation and deprivation of nationality.

The EURAs of Pakistan, Armenia and Azerbaijan outline in their Annexes 'Joint Declarations' of relevance for these situations. The EURA with Pakistan presents a Joint Declaration stating that the Parties take note that "according to the current Pakistan Citizenship Act, 1951,..., a citizen of Pakistan cannot renounce his citizenship without having acquired or having been given a valid document assuring the grant of citizenship or nationality of another State". The Declaration specifies that the parties agree to consult each other when the need arises. The EURA with Armenia presents a Joint Declaration related to cases of deprivation of nationality. It outlines that in accordance with the nationality law of Armenia and the EU Member States "it is not possible for a citizen of the Republic of Armenia or the European Union to be deprived of his or her nationality".[24] A similar Declaration has been introduced in the EURA with Azerbaijan which however no longer refers to the impossibility for EU Member States and EU citizens to be deprived of their citizenship.[25]

The EURAs foresee specific procedures for the issuing of a travel document in the scope of the article dedicated in the agreements on "Readmission of Nationals or Own Nationals". The EURA with Pakistan states in rather general terms that "The Requested state shall, as necessary and without delay, issue the person whose readmission has been accepted with the travel document required for his or her readmission, which shall be valid for at least six months".[26] That same article emphasizes that in cases where legal or factual obstacles are encountered so that the person involved cannot be transferred within the period of validity of the travel document, Pakistan shall issue a new travel document with the same period of validity within 14 days. This article has been fine-tuned in the EURAs that have subsequently been negotiated, as described below. Indeed, as Annex of this book

---

[23]Refer to Articles 2.2 in the EURA with Georgia and Cape Verde, and Article 3.2 of the EURA with Armenia, Azerbaijan and Turkey.

[24]Joint Declaration concerning Articles 3.3 and 5.3 EURA with Armenia. The Declaration adds that "The Parties agree to consult each other in due time should this legal situation change".

[25]Joint Declaration concerning Article 3.3 "The Contracting Parties take not that, according to the nationality laws of the Republic of Azerbaijan, it is not possible for a citizen of the Republic of Azerbaijan to be deprived of his or her nationality. The Parties agree to consult each other in due time, should this legal situation change".

[26]Article 2.2 of the Agreement.

illustrates, EURAs envisage specific time-limits for readmission procedures. It is therefore striking the information provided by the EMN (2014) highlighted above that "in the exceptional case of the EURA with Pakistan, it can take over a year to obtain a response from the authorities". This would mean that Article 8 of the EURA with Pakistan is being violated.[27]

The EURA with Georgia introduced the obligation for the competent authority to be the diplomatic mission or consular office, and for it to issue a travel document required for the return for a period of validity of 90 days "after Georgia has given a positive reply to the readmission application".[28] This provision continues by saying that this will take place "irrespective of the will of the person to be readmitted" immediately and no later than within 3 working days, otherwise the Agreement foresees that Georgia will be deemed to accept the EU standard travel document for expulsion purposes.

A similar article has been introduced in all the subsequent EURAs with few variations. The EURAs with Armenia and Azerbaijan add to that rule that the travel document will be free of charge. The EURAs with Cape Verde and Azerbaijan foresee different deadlines for the issuing of the travel document by the third country after given a positive reply to the readmission application, four and five working days respectively. There are also some differences concerning the period of validity of the travel documents, which ranges from 120 days in the EURA with Cape Verde, 150 days in the EURA with Azerbaijan and three months in the case of the EURA with Turkey. The EURA with Turkey has introduced an important new component in the operability of this procedure. According to Article 3.4 of this agreement, if Turkey does not comply with the three working days deadline, "the reply to the readmission application shall be considered as the necessary travel document for the readmission of the person concerned".

In those cases where there are legal or factual reasons preventing the transfer of the person, the subsequent EURAs under analysis include similar clauses to the one previously mentioned in the EURA with Pakistan. The main differences relate to decreasing the time within which a new travel document will need to be issued; which range from three working days in the EURAs with Georgia, Armenia and Turkey, to four working days in Cape Verde and five in the agreement with Azerbaijan.[29]

---

[27]Article 8.2 of the Agreement stipulates that "A readmission application must be replied to without undue delay, and in any event within a maximum of 30 calendar days; reasons shall be given for refusal of a readmission application. This time limit begins to run from the date of receipt of the readmission application. Where there are legal or factual obstacles to the application being replied to in time, the time limit may, upon request and giving reasons, be extended up to 60 calendar days, except if the maximum detention period in the national legislation of the Requesting State is less than, or equal to, 60 days. Where there is no reply within this time limit, the transfer shall be deemed to have been agreed to."

[28]Article 2.4 of the agreement.

[29]Article 2.5 in the EURAs with Georgia and Cape Verde, and Article 3.5 in EURAs with Armenia, Azerbaijan and Turkey.

4.2 Readmission Procedures: Principles and Means of Evidence

4.2.1 Principles

All EURAs include one Section dedicated to 'Readmission Procedures' which includes articles covering the principles to guide the readmission procedure, specific rules of the readmission application, a provision on the means of evidence regarding the nationality of the person to be readmitted, TCNs and stateless persons as well as time limits and transfer modalities. For the purposes of this book, it is of particular relevance to compare the general principles and the means of evidence of nationality in the Agreements under assessment.

Concerning the principles guiding readmission procedures, the EURAs lay down the obligation for the Requesting state to issue a readmission application to the competent authority of the requested state. Exemptions applicable to that obligation include cases when the person holds a valid travel document, visa and/residence authorisation of the requested state. Small variations have been included in the subsequent EURAs regarding the documents. For example the EURAs with Georgia and Cape Verde include "or identity card". Importantly, the EURA with Pakistan states: "No person shall be readmitted only on the basis of prima facie evidence of nationality." The EURA with Turkey provides a new feature in comparison to the previous five EURAs analysed in this study. Article 7.1 (Principles) states: "The Member States and Turkey shall make every effort to return a person directly to the country of origin."[30] This accompanies a Joint Declaration on Article 7.1 stating:

> The Parties agree that in order to demonstrate 'every effort to return a person referred to in Articles 4 and 6 directly to the country of origin', the Requesting State, while submitting a readmission application to the Requested State, should at the same time submit a readmission application also to the country of origin. The Requested State shall reply within the time limits mentioned in Article 11(2). The Requesting State informs the Requested State if a positive reply to the readmission application has been received from the country of origin in the meantime. In case where the country of origin of the person in question could not be determined and therefore a readmission application could not be submitted to the country of origin, the reasons of this situation should be stated in the readmission application which will be submitted to the Requested State.

---

[30]The EURA with Cape Verde and Azerbaijan include Joint Declarations covering precisely this same point. Refer to Joint Declaration concerning Articles 3 and 5 in the EURA Cape Verde which states that "The Contracting Parties will endeavour to return any third country national who does not, or who no longer, fulfils the legal conditions in force for entry to, presence in or residence on their respective territories, to his or her country of origin." See also Joint Declaration in the EURA with Azerbaijan which reads as follows "The Parties will endeavour to return any third country national who does not, or who no longer, fulfils the legal conditions for entry to, presence or residence to his/her country of origin".

Table 4.2 EURA with Pakistan: documents furnishing nationality or initiating the process of establishing nationality

Evidence of nationality	Documents initiating the process of establishing nationality
Genuine Passports of any kind (national passports, diplomatic passports, service passports, collective passports and surrogate passports including children's passports)	Digital fingerprints or other biometric data
Computerised national identity cards	Temporary and provisional national identity cards, military identity cards and birth certificates issued by the Government of the requested party
Genuine citizenship certificates	Photocopies (officially authenticated by the authorities of Pakistan) of other official documents that mention or indicate citizenship (e.g. birth certificates)
	Service cards, seaman's registration cards, skipper's service cards or photocopies thereof
	Statements made by the person concerned

Source Author's own elaboration

4.2.2 Means of Evidence of Nationality

A particularly important common provision in the six EURAs relates to the means of evidence for determining the person's nationality. The provision needs to be read in conjunction with Annexes attached to the EURAs dealing with common lists of document the presentation of which is to be considered as evidence or *prima facie* evidence of nationality/citizenship for the purposes of the Agreements. The EURA with Pakistan provides that proof of nationality may be furnished through the list of documents comprised in Annex I of the Agreement, "even if their period of validity has expired". If those documents are presented both parties "shall mutually recognize the nationality without further investigation required".[31] The Agreement further stipulates that proof of nationality can be also furnished through additional documents "the presentation of which shall initiate the process for establishing nationality" as laid down in Annex II. It is provided that when these documents are presented "the Requested State shall initiate the process of establishing the nationality of the person concerned". Table 4.2 outlines the list of documents which are presumed to proof nationality or prima facie nationality in the EURA with Pakistan.

Annex of this book provides a detailed overview of the ways in which the annexes in the six EURAs under assessment deal with documents that are deemed to constitute evidence or *prima facie* evidence of nationality. As stated above, the EURA with Pakistan is clear in stating that no person will be readmitted on the

---

[31] Refer to Article 6.2 of the EURA with Pakistan.

4.2 Readmission Procedures: Principles and Means of Evidence

basis of 'prima facie' evidence of nationality.[32] This constitutes a fundamental difference in comparison to all the subsequent EURAs, which have expanded the ways in which nationality or *prima facie* nationality are presumed for the purposes of readmission. As Table 4.3 clearly illustrates, the EURA with Pakistan is comparably the agreement presenting a stringent list of documents that are deemed to be acceptable for verifying nationality of the person to be readmitted, or the presentation of which initiates the process of establishing nationality.

The EURA with Georgia provides an Annex II titled 'Common List of Documents the presentation of which is considered as *prima facie* evidence of nationality' and expressly states in Article 8 that "if such documents are presented, the Member States and Georgia shall consider the nationality to be established" for the purpose of readmission unless it can be proved otherwise". Furthermore, when it comes to the specific list of documents which are deemed *prima facie* proof of nationality, the EURA with Georgia contains a more developed list than the one foreseen with Pakistan, including the possibility of accepting the documents listed in Annex I whose validity has expired by more than 6 months, but also "any other documents such as driving licenses, company cards, laissez-passer issued by the Requested state, "any other document which may help to establish the nationality of the person concerned." It also includes the presumption of nationality resulting from a search in the Visa Information System (VIS) or national visa information systems for those EU Member States not part of Schengen system.

The EURAs with Armenia, Cape Verde, Azerbaijan and Turkey follow a similar model as the one negotiated with Georgia. They present some variations and new features however that are worth underlining when comparing the list documents provided in the same Annexes I and II of the Agreements. The EURAs with Cape Verde and Turkey are the two Agreements accepting a larger list of documents as proof of nationality. They include documents which in the other EURAs under examination are only foreseen *as prima facie* evidence. For instance, in addition to those established in the EURA with Pakistan, the EURA with Cape Verde accepts as proof of nationality documents such as *laissez-passer* issued by the Requested state, service books and military identity cards, seamen's registration books and skippers service cards.[33] The EURA with Turkey similarly accepts those extra documents as proof of nationality. It can been seen as the agreement providing a wider list of documents aimed at proving the nationality of the person to be expelled among the ones covered in this Report. The agreements with Georgia, Armenia and Azerbaijan only accept these same documents as *prima facie* evidence.

When it comes to the common list of documents considered as *prima facie* evidence of nationality, as illustrated in Table 4.3, some variations can be noticed when comparing the six EURAs. The EURA with Pakistan is the only one expressly stating that "digital fingerprints or other biometric data" are accepted. The

---

[32] Article 4 of the EURA with Pakistan.

[33] The EURA with Azerbaijan in Annex I accepts as a proof of nationality identity cards of any kind "with the exception of seaman's identity cards".

Table 4.3 Documenting legal and functional identity—EURAs compared

	Pakistan	Georgia	Armenia	Cape Verde	Azerbaijan	Turkey
Passport	X	X	X	X	X	X
National identity card	X	X	X	X	X	X
Birth certificate	N.A.	≈	N.A.	≈	≈	≈
Temporary identity card and birth certificate	≈	N.A.	X	X	X	X
Citizenship certificates	X	X	X	X	X	X
Other document clearly indicating citizenship	≈	X	X	X	N.A.	X
Photocopies	≈	≈	N.A.	N.A.	N.A.	≈
Expired documents	N.A.	≈	≈	N.A.	≈	≈
Digital Fingerprints	≈	N.A.	≈	≈	≈	N.A.
Biometrics	≈	N.A.	N.A.	N.A.	N.A.	N.A.
Entry/exist registration system	N.A.	N.A.	N.A.	N.A.	≈	N.A.
Seaman identity card/registration books	≈	≈	≈	X	≈	X
Skipper service card	N.A.	N.A.	N.A.	X	≈	X
Laissez-passer	N.A.	≈	≈	X	X	X
Service books/military identity cards	≈	≈	≈	X	≈	X
EU visa information system/national visa database	N.A.	≈	≈	X	≈	X
Statement by person concerned	≈	≈	≈	≈	≈	≈
Statement by witnesses	N.A.	N.A.	≈	≈	≈	≈
Spoken language/language test	N.A.	≈	≈	≈	≈	≈
Driving licence	N.A.	≈	N.A.	≈	≈	≈
Company identity card	N.A.	≈	≈	≈	≈	≈
Documents with pictures replacing passport	N.A.	N.A.	N.A.	N.A.	N.A.	≈
Any other document	N.A.	≈	≈	≈	≈	≈

Legend X Evidence of Nationality, ≈ Prima Facie Evidence, N.A. Not Applicable
Source Author's own elaboration

EURAs with Armenia, Cape Verde and Azerbaijan only refer to fingerprints. In respect of information systems, the EURAs with Georgia and Armenia expressly mention the VIS, and national visa information systems in those EU Member States not participating in VIS. In the case of Azerbaijan, this also includes "confirmation of identity as a result of a search carried out in IAMAS (Entry-Exist and Registration Automated Information System of the Republic of Azerbaijan)". Other means of *prima facie* proof of nationality include statements by witnesses in the EURA with Armenia, Cape Verde, Azerbaijan and Turkey; or statements and/or written account of statements made by the person concerned and language spoken, including by means of an official language test.

The EURA also foresee procedures for those cases where none of these documents exist. The EURA with Pakistan states in rather general terms that the competent authorities will make the necessary arrangements to interview the person concerned "without undue delay". Similarly, the other five EURAs set specific deadlines for this interview to take place; specifically ranging between three to five working days in the EURAs with Armenia, Azerbaijan, Cape Verde and Georgia, to seven in the EURA with Turkey.[34] All EURAs, with the exception of the one with Pakistan, highlight that the procedures applicable to the interviews will be laid down in 'Implementing Protocols', which we analyse in the following subsection.

4.2.3 Application and Implementation

All EURAs under examination foresee a Section dedicated to 'Implementation and Application'. A key provision comprising these Sections relates to 'Implementing Protocols', which are bilateral in nature and fundamentals.[35] Article 20 of the EURA with Pakistan emphasizes that Pakistan and a Member State may draw up an implementing Protocol covering the designation of the competent authorities, border crossing points and exchange of contact points, conditions for escorted returns and means and documents other than those listed in Annexes I and II. The other five EURAs present a number of commonalities and specificities when compared to the one with Pakistan.

---

[34] Article 9 of the EURA with Turkey stipulates that "In case there are no diplomatic or consular representations of the Requested State in the Requesting State, the former shall make the necessary arrangements in order to interview the person to be readmitted without undue delay, at the latest within seven working days from the requesting day. The procedure for such interviews may be established in the implementing Protocols provided for in Article 20 of this Agreement."

[35] According to the European Commission (2011), "The Commission (with strong support from the MS) has always insisted that the EURAs are self-standing, directly operational instruments which do not necessarily require the conclusion of bilateral implementing protocols with the third country. In the longer term protocols are mere facilitators, even if they are sometimes mandatory, as in the EURA with Russia", p. 4.

Since the EURA with Georgia, all subsequent EURAs provide that the Implementing Protocols may also include the modalities for readmission under accelerated procedures and the above-mentioned procedures for interviews in cases where there are no documents proving nationality. The only obligation foreseen for the validity of the Implementing Protocols is that they will enter into force" only after the Committee has been notified. Furthermore, the EURA with Georgia states that "Georgia agrees to apply any provision of an implementing Protocol drawn up with one Member States also in its relation with any other Member State upon request of the latter". A similar provision is included in Article 19 of the EURA with Cape Verde. In a different fashion, the EURA with Armenia provides: "The Member States agree to apply any provision of an implementing Protocol concluded by one of them also in their relations with Armenia upon request of the latter, subject to practical feasibility of its application to other Member States". A similar provision is foreseen in Article 20 of the EURA with Azerbaijan. Implementing Protocols remain confidential in nature and are not disclosed to the public.

In addition to Implementing Protocols, the EURAs Section on 'Implementation and Application' also foresees a key instrument that has been devised to ensure 'effectiveness' in the implementation of each specific EURA. The EURA model foresees the establishment of a so-called Joint Readmission Committee (JRC) with the competence of monitoring the uniform application of the agreement in question, address questions related to its interpretation or practical application, proposing changes or amendments to its provisions and exchange relevant information. JRC decisions are binding on the parties to the Agreement, with the exception of the EURA with Pakistan.[36] They are composed by representatives of the EU (represented by the European Commission and Member States' experts) and the third country concerned. It follows its own Rules of Procedure. Decisions and operational arrangements agreed by JRC are also confidential. In contrast to the previous EURAs under study, the EURA with Turkey includes a new feature or requirements regarding the validity of the decisions by the JRC.

Open Access This chapter is distributed under the terms of the Creative Commons Attribution 4.0 International License (http://creativecommons.org/licenses/by/4.0/), which permits use, duplication, adaptation, distribution and reproduction in any medium or format, as long as you give appropriate credit to the original author(s) and the source, a link is provided to the Creative Commons license and any changes made are indicated.

The images or other third party material in this chapter are included in the work's Creative Commons license, unless indicated otherwise in the credit line; if such material is not included in the work's Creative Commons license and the respective action is not permitted by statutory regulation, users will need to obtain permission from the license holder to duplicate, adapt or reproduce the material.

---

[36]A key difference has been introduced in the EURA with Turkey which says in Article 19.2 that it is binding "following any necessary internal procedures required by the law of the Contracting Parties".

References

Agreement between the European Union and Turkey on the readmission of persons residing without authorization OJ L 134/3 7 May 2014

Agreement between the European Union and the Republic of Azerbaijan on the readmission of persons residing without authorization OJ L 128/17 30 Apr 2014

Agreement between the European Union and the Republic of Cape Verde on the readmission of persons residing without authorization OJ L 282/15 24 Oct 2013

Agreement between the European Union and the Republic of Armenia on the readmission of persons residing without authorization OJ L 289/13 31 Oct 2013

Agreement between the European Union and Georgia on the readmission of persons residing without authorization OJ L 52/47 25 Feb 2011

Agreement between the European Community and the Islamic Republic of Pakistan on the readmission of persons residing without authorisation OJ L 287/52 4 Nov 2010

Agreement between the European Community and the Republic of Serbia on the readmission of persons residing without authorisation OJ L 334/46 19 Dec 2007

Agreement between the European Community and the Republic of Montenegro on the readmission of persons residing without authorization OJ L 334/26 19 Dec 2007

Agreement between the European Community and Bosnia and Herzegovina on the readmission of persons residing without authorization OJ L 334/66 19 Dec 2007

Agreement between the European Community and the Republic of Moldova on the readmission of persons residing without authorisation OJ L 334/149 19 Dec 2007

Agreement between the European Community and Ukraine on the readmission of persons OJ L 332/48 18 Dec 2007

Agreement between the European Community and the former Yugoslav Republic of Macedonia on the readmission of persons residing without authorization OJ L 334/7 19 Dec 2007

Agreement between the European Community and the Russian Federation on readmission OJ L 129/40 17 May 2007

Agreement between the European Community and the Republic of Albania on the readmission of persons residing without authorization OJ L 124/22 17 May 2005

Agreement between the European Community and the Democratic Socialist Republic of Sri Lanka on the readmission of persons residing without authorization OJ L 124/43 17 May 2005

Agreement between the European Community and the Macao Special Administrative Region of the People's Republic of China on the readmission of persons residing without authorization OJ L 143/99 30 Apr 2004

Agreement between the European Community and the Government of the Hong Kong Special Administrative Region of the People's Republic of China on the readmission of persons residing without authorization OJ L 17/25 24 Jan 2004

Council of the EU (2002) Criteria for the identification of third countries with which new readmission agreements need to be negotiated. 7990/02, Brussels, 16 Apr 2002

European Commission (2011) Evaluation of EU readmission agreements. COM (2011) 76, 23 Feb 2011

Chapter 5
The Implementation Challenges and Dynamics of EURAs

This Chapter examines the challenges affecting the implementation of EURAs once entered into force. Particular attention is paid to the challenges emerging from the identity determination dilemma explained and substantiated in Chap. 3 above. These include: first, lack of accountability and transparency (Sect. 5.1); second, the value added of EU intervention; (Sect. 5.2) third, inter-state and sovereign relations challenges (Sect. 5.3); and fourth, the blurring of rights and the agency of the individual (Sect. 5.4).

5.1 Lack of Accountability and Transparency

The criteria identified by the Council of the EU for justifying the need to conclude EURAs with third countries include cases where such an agreement would 'add value' to EU Member States bilateral negotiations and expulsion practices, including cases where there are "relevant obstacles to return, in particular in what concerns obtaining travel documents for the repatriation of people who do not fulfil or no longer fulfil entry or residence conditions.[1] How to measure this 'value' precisely when it comes to expulsion outcomes? A first challenge in examining the 'effectiveness' in the implementation of EURAs relates to the lack of transparency and accountability of the exact ways in which these legal instruments operate in practice, as well as regarding the implementing procedures that put them into effect.

As Chap. 2 above has illustrated, the way in which the European Commission and EU Member States currently measure 'effectiveness' is a predominantly numerical exercise comparing removal orders and enforced return rates. What do the official statistics tell us about the state of expulsions of irregular immigrants in the EU? According to EUROSTAT, and as outlined in Graph 5.1 and Table 5.1,

---

[1] Council of the EU (2002).

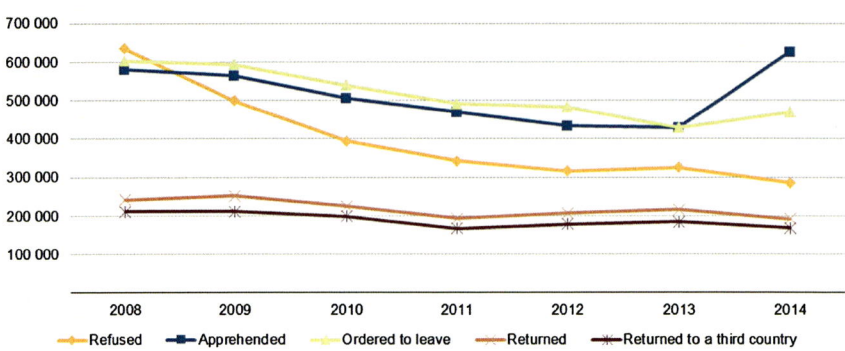

Graph 5.1 TCNs subject to the enforcement of immigration legislation in EU. *Source* Eurostat (http://ec.europa.eu/eurostat/statistics-explained/index.php/Statistics_on_enforcement_of_immigration_legislation Accessed 8 June 2016)

Table 5.1 Total number of TCNs ordered to leave and returns EU-28 2008–2014

	2008	2009	2010	2011	2012	2013	2014
TCNs returned to a third country	211,350	211,785	198,910	167,150	178,500	184,765	168,925
TCNs ordered to leave	603,360	594,600	540,080	491,310	483,650	430,450	470,080

Source Eurostat (http://ec.europa.eu/eurostat/statistics-explained/index.php/Statistics_on_enforcement_of_immigration_legislation Accessed 8 June 2016)

over 470,000 third-country nationals were issued with an 'order to leave' or removal order in an EU Member State in 2014. Only 36 % of these were returned to a non-EU country (168,925).

EUROSTAT data also tell us that the total number of removal orders and returns of TCNs, outlined in Graph 5.2, have remained by and large stable and in a decreasing trend since 2008.

A similar tendency can be identified in some countries with which the EU has concluded an EURA, in particular among the six under assessment in this book (see Table 5.2). As a way of illustration, the statistics on Pakistan, Georgia and Armenia (which are the only countries whose EURA has entered into force respectively in 2010 and 2011) do not show an increase of returns since the entry into force of the agreements with the EU.[2] The fact that countries with which the EU has a readmission agreement are the main sources of irregular immigration into the EU tell us

---

[2]As illustrated in Chap. 2 above, the other four EURAs with Armenia, Cape Verde, Azerbaijan and Turkey only entered into force in 2014 and therefore it is too early to assess any impact of the Agreement on the number of removal orders and returns.

5.1 Lack of Accountability and Transparency

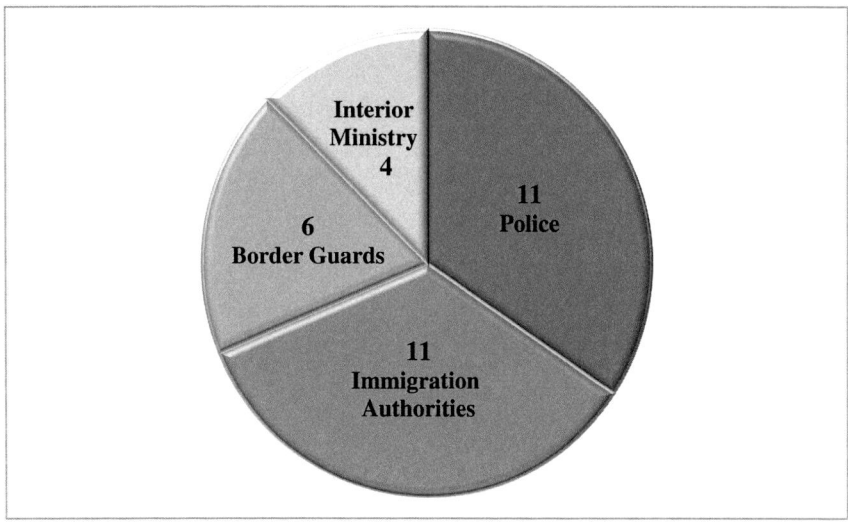

Graph 5.2 EU member states authorities responsible for implementing EURAs. *Source* Author's own elaboration based on EMN (2014)

little about the effectiveness of its use in comparison to other third countries where such EURAs do not exist. This picture does not substantiate the above-mentioned Commission's argument that the conclusion of an EURA has resulted in an increased number of expulsions. It is therefore not at all clear what actual 'impact' the operation of an EURA has had in practice.

The quantitative picture provided by EUROSTAT tells us little about the nature, applied legal framework, scope and effects of expulsion practices of irregular and undocumented immigrants by EU Member States. EUROSTAT explains that the substantive variations identified across EU Member States when it comes to removal orders and expulsions can be understood due to "disparities in migration policies, as well as administrative, statistical and legal (legal acts, judicial procedure, etc.) among EU Member States."[3] It is difficult to drawn conclusive findings or results from this statistical coverage and aggregated figures.

---

[3]Refer to http://ec.europa.eu/eurostat/statistics-explained/index.php/Statistics_on_enforcement_of_immigration_legislation Accessed 31 May 2016. Eurostat explains that the concept of "Third country nationals ordered to leave" incudes "Third country nationals found to be illegally present who are subject to an administrative or judicial decision or act stating that their stay is illegal and imposing an obligation to leave the territory of the Member State (see Article 7.1 (a) of the Regulation). These statistics do not include persons who are transferred from one Member State to another under the mechanism established by the Dublin Regulation. Each person is counted only once within the reference period, irrespective of the number of notices issued to the same person. Moreover, the following notion of "Third country nationals returned following an order to leave" is given: "Third country nationals who have in fact left the territory of the Member State, following an administrative or judicial decision or act stating that their stay is illegal and imposing an

Table 5.2 Total returns and removal orders EU 28 2008–2014 to selected third countries

Pakistan	2008	2009	2010	2011	2012	2013	2014
TCNs returned	4.420	4.840	5.270	7.970	13.565	11.230	6.705
TCNs ordered to leave	16.860	16.660	20.160	32.255	35.460	25.360	21.210
Georgia							
TCNs returned	1.715	2.225	3.080	2.240	2.815	3.250	3.503
TCNs ordered to leave	6.445	8.170	6.855	4.325	5.645	6.030	6.235
Armenia							
TCNs returned	1.350	1.035	1.100	1.235	1.340	1.230	1.205
TCNs ordered to leave	3.490	3.510	4.005	5.390	5.230	6.015	5.195
Cape Verde							
TCNs returned	285	230	250	270	285	240	230
TCNs ordered to leave	1.270	1.505	1.455	1.645	1.695	1.745	1.250
Azerbaijan							
TCNs returned	535	505	455	490	540	535	520
TCNs ordered to leave	1.185	1.130	1.260	1.295	1.330	1.485	1.235
Turkey							
TCNs returned	8.430	6.735	5.380	4.890	3.980	3.440	2.940
TCNs ordered to leave	15.705	15.180	11.885	10.940	10.635	10.320	9.910

*Entry into force of EURA
Source Author's own compilation based on data provided by Eurostat

There are a number of methodological caveats inherent to the available data as reported by EU Member States. These include for instance no clear indications as regards which expulsions have taken place inside or outside the scope of EURAs or other bilateral (formal and/or informal) frameworks and tools of cooperation. The statistics do not specify either the total number of EURA readmission requests which have been approved or refused by EU Member State concerned, the reasons of refusal or the number of travel documents issued for which countries of origin. Neither do they outline the total number of requests for travel documents in the

---

(Footnote 3 continued)

obligation to leave the territory. On a voluntary basis Member States provide Eurostat with a subcategory which relates to third country nationals returned to a third country only. Persons who left the territory within the year may have been subject to an obligation to leave in a previous year. As such, the number of persons who actually left the territory may be greater than those who were subject to an obligation to leave in the same year."

5.1 Lack of Accountability and Transparency

context of EURAs and those which have been granted by the third countries concerned or requested.

The Commission has concluded that EURA are rarely used for 'voluntary returns'.[4] The removal orders and return rates reported by Eurostat do not however differentiate between those that have been 'voluntary' or 'forced'; neither do they clarify whether the individuals are persons having received a negative decision on asylum applications or irregular immigrants or undocumented.[5] Not every TCN who is returned is always served with an order to leave or removal order in all EU Member States, especially in those cases of 'voluntary returns'.[6] There is neither statistical coverage concerning detention of TCNs in the EU, or on what happens to people during and after the expulsion procedure.[7]

The resulting scene is one preventing a proper assessment and understanding of the implementation of EURAs. The difficulty in assessing the value added of EURA in expulsion procedures from a purely numerical perspective is exacerbated by a high degree of secrecy when it comes to the ways in which EURAs foresee their application and implementation procedures which have been described in Chap. 4 above. The role attributed to JRC and Implementing Protocols are of central importance in all the EURAs. That notwithstanding, all the decisions and internal deliberations in the scope of JRC specific to each EURA are not publicly available or disclosed.[8] This is the case despite the fundamental importance of the decisions and discussions taking place in these Committees when it relates to: first, decisions amending the wording and procedural specifications of a particular EURA, including practical arrangements for conducting interviews for determining nationality in cases where the person involved is undocumented or in cases of accelerated procedures; and second, ways to address specific practical challenges affecting the correct application of the agreement in question, such as the EURA with Pakistan.

---

[4]European Commission (2011).

[5]According to Eurostat "Starting with first reference year 2014 new statistics on third country returnee were as well collected by Eurostat on voluntary basis." See http://ec.europa.eu/eurostat/cache/metadata/en/migr_eil_esms.htm.

[6]Cassarino (2010) p. 47.

[7]Singleton (2016).

[8]The author of this book made an official request for access to documents to the Commission (DG Migration and Home Affairs) to have access to the Operational Conclusions adopted in the Joint Readmission Committee meeting of 2 February 2016, relating to EU Readmission Agreement with Pakistan. Access was rejected by the Commission in a letter of 6 June 2016. The application was not granted on the basis that "it has been agreed with the Pakistani side that records and other documents of the Joint Readmission Committee shall be treated confidentially. Therefore, we consider that disclosing such information would jeopardise our current and future relations with Pakistan within the Joint Readmission Committee and would be detrimental to keeping a good and fruitful negotiating position with Pakistan in a highly sensitive file. Thus, disclosure would undermine the protection of public interest as regards international relations, as laid down in the provision of the Regulation 1049/2001 referred to above."

Chapter 4 above has showed how important the adoption of Implementing Protocols to EURAs can be. These Protocols are bilateral in nature, and, depending on the specific EURA in question, may be applicable to other EU Member States. Their importance resides in their role of designing and fleshing out the modalities for readmission under accelerated procedures and procedures applicable to interviews in cases where there are no documents proving nationality. The only requirement foreseen by EURAs as regards the Implementing Protocols is their notification to the relevant JRC. Similarly to JRC decisions, the number of EU Member States having concluded Implementing Protocols in the scope of EURAs and the texts of these Protocols are not publicly accessible. Table 5.3 shows a full list of Implementing Protocols which have been concluded between EU Member States and third countries in the scope of all existing EU Readmission Agreements. The exact content of these protocols remains confidential. It is noticeable that in the EURA with Pakistan only the UK counts with an Implementing Protocol. The only publicly available information about them has been provided by a couple of studies by the EMN in 2014 on the basis of responses by Member States' national contact points. The EMN study on "Good Practices in the Return and Reintegration of Irregular Migrants: Member States" Entry Bans Policies and use of readmission agreements between Member States and Third Countries' stated:

> By 2012 most Member States (Austria, Belgium, Bulgaria, Czech Republic, Estonia, Germany, Greece, Finland, France, Hungary, Lithuania, Luxembourg, Latvia, Netherlands, Poland, Portugal, Romania, Slovenia, Spain) and Norway had applied implementing protocols concluded under EU Readmission Agreements with third countries and in 2013, protocols to support the implementation of EU readmission agreements entered into force in three Member States (Hungary, Slovakia and the UK).[9]

5.2 The Value Added of Formal and Informal EU Readmission Instruments

This lack of transparency undermines any attempt to gain an understanding of the contribution and value added of EURAs in sending people back when compared to already existing formal and informal bilateral readmission instruments, clauses and agreements by EU Member States. The academic literature has documented and analyzed the turf wars between the European Commission and some EU Member States as regards the reach and scope of legal competence at times of concluding readmission instruments with countries with which the EU has a EURA.[10]

---

[9]EMN (2014) p. 21.
[10]Peers et al. (2012).

5.2 The Value Added of Formal and Informal EU Readmission Instruments

Table 5.3 List of implementing protocols in EURAs

	Bosnia and Herzegovina	Montenegro	Former Yugoslav Republic of Macedonia	Serbia	Albania	Moldova	Russia	Ukraine	Sri Lanka	Hong Kong	Macao	Pakistan	Georgia	Armenia	Azerbaijan	Turkey
BE		X			X		X									
BG		X	X	X	X	X	X						X			
CZ	X	X		X		X	X	X								
EE	X	X	X	X		X	X						X			
FI							X									
FR				X	X		X									
IE																
IT		X		X	X	X	X									
CY				X		X	X						X			
LT						X	X									
LV						X	X									
LX		X			X		X									
HU					X	X	X						X			
MT	X	X		X	X	X	X									
DE	X	X	X	X	X	X	X			X						
NL		X			X		X									
PL						X	X									
PT				X	X		X									
AT	X	X	X	X	X	X	X	X					X			
RO				X		X	X									
EL																
SK	X	X	X	X	X	X	X						X			
SI		X		X			X									

(continued)

Table 5.3 (continued)

	Bosnia and Herzegovina	Montenegro	Former Yugoslav Republic of Macedonia	Serbia	Albania	Moldova	Russia	Ukraine	Sri Lanka	Hong Kong	Macao	Pakistan	Georgia	Armenia	Azerbaijan	Turkey
ES						x	x									
SE				x			x									
UK				x								x				
HR																

Source European Commission (This table was provided by DG Migration and Home Affairs of the Commission in answer to a request for access to documents made by the author of this book on 6 June 2016)

5.2 The Value Added of Formal and Informal EU Readmission Instruments

Article 79.3 of the Treaty on the Functioning of the European Union (TFEU) provides express legal mandate for the Union to conclude EURAs, and Article 218 TFEU stipulates the procedures for their conclusion. The European Commission is required to ask the Council for a mandate to negotiate with the third country concerned. DG Home Affairs is in the driver's seat of the negotiations of the initial text of the agreement which will need to be adopted by the Council and receive the consent by the European Parliament. The issuing of the negotiating mandate/directives by the Council is irrespective of the actual interest or willingness by the third country concerned to even enter into any sort of negotiations with the Commission in the matter (European Commission 2011).[11] This has caused severe friction and repeated pressures from EU Member States on the Commission to ease and hasten negotiations for the agreements.

Of particular concern in this discussion has been the expansive use of informal paths of cooperation and policy instruments between some EU Member States and third countries, which too often escape the decision-making procedures envisaged by the EU Treaties, as well as proper democratic accountability and judicial oversight. In its 2011 evaluation of EURAs the Commission stated that "The Member States need to apply EURAs for all their returns. The Commission will closely monitor the correct implementation of EURAs by Member States and, if necessary, consider legal steps in case of incorrect or lack of implementation".[12] In response to the 2015–2016 'European refugee crisis', it seems that a similar working logic of informality on readmission deals and instruments is now being promoted and developed by the EU. As noted in Chap. 2 above, some European institutions are favouring the use of informal (including bilateral) arrangements or patterns of cooperation on readmission with third countries for the sake of increasing expulsion rates.

Informal and non-legally binding instruments covering readmission in the scope of High-Level Migration Dialogues of the EU may be deemed to facilitate negotiations with third countries, especially those unwilling or lacking interest in concluding a formal and publicly visible EURA. Interviews carried out as background to this book have clarified that one of the main purposes behind these informal methods of cooperation primarily aim at finding "the soft spot" in these third countries, i.e. the authority or actor which may be willing to cooperate in identity determination and/or issuing travel documents. EU officials have alluded to the lack of interest by third countries authorities to openly and publicly cooperate with the

---

[11] The Communication stated that "the negotiation of EURAs takes a very long time. A case in point is Morocco, where the negotiating directives were received in 2000, the first negotiating round took place in 2003 and negotiations are currently in their 15th round with little prospect of a swift conclusion. In addition, in two cases (China and Algeria) the EU has not even managed to formally open negotiations", Ibid.

[12] Ibid. p. 4.

Union on readmission and identification issues of their own nationals (chiefly through the conclusion of a EURA) due to its lack of popularity in domestic populations as well as Diasporas in EU Member States. This stands in sharp contradiction with the EU's growing appetite to widely disseminate and openly publicize the 'success' of readmission when it comes to increasing expulsion rates of irregular immigrants. The soft spot working logic constitutes in this way an excellent example of 'venue shopping' in the development of EU external migration law and policy.[13] EU actors 'go abroad' through the use of new (formal and informal/bilateral and multilateral) readmission instruments, or attributing new functionalities to previously existing ones, in an attempt to avoid legal (rule of law) constraints and find new co-operating parties or new allies.

The dilemmas inherent in EU actions to cooperate with third countries to tackle irregular immigration were acknowledged by the Commission Communication on the work of the so-called "Task Force Mediterranean", which stated: "Relations with partner countries will also have to take into account the specific sensitivities and expectations of partner countries on the migration dossier, and their perception that the EU wishes to focus primarily on security-related aspects, readmission/ return and the fight against irregular migration" (European Commission 2013). As Carrera and Guild have previously argued "for these third countries, [EU-driven] security-related aspects may be interpreted as an allegation that their citizens are potential criminals; Readmission and return may be understood as meaning that their own citizens are framed as 'illegal immigrants'; and the EU's fight against irregular migration could mean that they should take measures for their citizens not to go on holiday to the EU".[14]

Political (non-legally binding) and often secretive documents are also preferred by some authorities in these third countries in an attempt not to subject the issue to public light and domestic debates. That notwithstanding, these informalities do not properly address, and arguably may even exacerbate, the practical implementation challenges of states' commitments related to identification and issuing of travel documents to own nationals examined in this book. A noticeable example may be the *Pham* case studied in Sect. 3.2 above, which has occurred despite the existence

---

[13]Guiraudon (2000) has argued that 'venue shopping' constituted one of the main motives behind policy making in European Union levels (the internationalization or vertical policy making) on 'migration control' and the development of the common EU immigration policy. By doing, she argued, it shifted policy elaboration away from national judiciaries. In her view "Yet migration control experts took advantage of new organizational setting not previously available to them. The 'wining and dining culture' of the 1970s Trevi Group alerted law and order ministries to the potential of European-wide scope of policy making. Once a model had been set for security 'clubs' that discussed drugs or terrorism, it was easy to add new types of working groups responsible for other cross-border issues or to widen the subject matter of a pre-existing one....migration control officials meeting their counterparts in the early 1980s established links between migration, asylum and crime-related issues, and emphasized technical issues that required their expertise", p. 260.

[14]Carrera and Guild (2014) pp. 10 and 11.

5.2 The Value Added of Formal and Informal EU Readmission Instruments

of a non-legally binding Memorandum of Understanding (MoU) on readmission between the UK and Vietnam since 2004.[15]

Informal patterns of cooperation and non-legally binding instruments including a readmission angle enhance the legal uncertainty and the lack of sufficient procedural guarantees designing inter-state challenges. What do they add in comparison to EURAs? It is not clear the extent to which non-binding informal arrangements and MoU complement or compete with formal EURAs. As the European Commission rightly pointed out in its 2011 evaluation of EURAs, the use of informal patterns of cooperation may make "More seriously, human rights and international protection guarantees in EURAs ineffective if MS do not return irregular migrants under EURAs."[16] Non-binding arrangements are equally contingent, compared to EURAs, on the state of diplomatic relations. This in turn will make ever more challenging the practical operability and sustainability of 'the rules of the game' in inter-state relations when it comes to readmission practices.

The above-mentioned 2016 Council Conclusions on the expulsions of illegally staying TCNs state: "Such legally non-binding arrangements should be fully compatible with existing bilateral readmission agreements of the Member States, and may in cases contribute to creating the conditions for the negotiation and conclusion of future readmission agreements as cooperation develops." It is not entirely clear how this compatibility will be ensured. The development of informal arrangements can be only expected to increase the inconsistencies and, arguably, further undermine the credibility of the EU's readmission policy. The non-legally binding nature will furthermore make them highly vulnerable and unstable to the state of diplomatic or inter-state relations. Some EU Member States' representatives have declared that one of the main contributions of EURAs has been not so much the increased number of removals, but rather the "benefits in terms of strengthening our bilateral relationships with other countries, including on practical cooperation efforts combating illegal immigration".[17] As the next section shows, however, EURAs are still fraught with profound inter-state and inter-actor controversies.

5.3 Inter-state and Inter-actor Challenges: Re-modelling the Boundaries of Authority

Scholars have documented and assessed the origins of inter-state relations and cooperation in the readmission of their own nationals, as well as the different types of readmission-related instruments and agreements that have progressively

---

[15]According to the EMN (2014) the UK and Vietnam signed a MoU on 28 October 2004. See Annex 2, Table A2.8, p. 47.
[16]Ibid.
[17]UK House of Commons (2013), paragraph 4.4.

developed in European cooperation, especially since the mid-1990s.[18] A central issue underlying this development has been the need to develop these formal and/or informal instruments and EU frameworks of cooperation on readmission in light of the general duty by states of origin to 'readmit' their own nationals. If states are under an obligation to readmit their nationals, why are readmission agreements necessary?

The duty of states to take back their nationals has been widely accepted as a key component in customary international law. The Court of Justice of the European Union (CJEU) held in the *Van Duyn v Home Office* (Case 41/74): "For a national, however undesirable and potentially harmful his entry may be, cannot be refused admission into his own state. A state has a duty under international law to receive back its own nationals".[19] In paragraph 22, the Court concluded: "it is a principle of international law, which the EEC Treaty cannot be assumed to disregard in the relations between Member States, that a State is precluded from refusing its own nationals the right of entry or residence."

What is lacking is a common understanding of the actual nature and fundamentals of that obligation in states practices.[20] There is no agreement on the ways in which that duty is to become operational in practical terms. Hailbronner has argued that "the obligation to readmit one's own nationals is the correlate to the right to expel aliens".[21] There is however not such a wide consensus as regards the actual scope of that obligation, and the extent to which it relates to the right to leave and return by individuals of these same states as enshrined in international human rights instruments.[22]

Irrespective of the discussion on 'the duty to readmit' by the country of origin, a key dilemma that leaves the implementation of EURAs unsettled is *who* is sovereign to determine who is a national of which country. EU Member States can try to substantiate the nationality of a person to be readmitted in various ways and forms. Yet, the procedure and resulting decision are by no means enforceable or have non international legal value, not least for the alleged or presumed country of origin or nationality. Irrespective of the success by states and later the EU in concluding legal and non-legal arrangements developing the particulars of the duty to readmit nationals, the question of 'whose citizen' is still the cause of ceaseless inter-state frictions.[23] In such a context, EURAs foresee a set of 'technical' procedures, rules and lists of documents intended to ease or facilitate the determination of who is to be considered a national of the country concerned, and which means of proof are

---

[18]Hailbronner (1997), Coleman (2009), Bouteillet-Paquet (2003).
[19]Case *Van Duyn v. Home Office* 41/74, 4 December 1974, p. 1345.
[20]Kruse (2006).
[21]Hailbronner (1997) p. 57.
[22]Goodwin-Gill (1975).
[23]Gregou (2014) has argued that "The incomplete expulsion procedure in these cases (Afghan, Iraqi and Pakistani nationals) could be attributable to the problematic cooperation with the countries of origin. The nationality and identity verification in cooperation in the diplomatic agencies of the country of origin, usually involve time-consuming procedures", p. 524.

considered to provide various degrees of proof of the persons' citizenship and consequent legal status. As Peers et al. have argued

> [Readmission agreements] are attractive to most Member States because no decision to expel a person can be effective unless another State agrees to take that person onto its territory, and most Member States believe that a formal treaty obligation will assist in accomplishing this objective...The agreements can be used to set out rules on means of "proof" and "evidence" to increase the prospect that the requested States will accept people back, and to include rules on transit through the requested State (not strictly speaking a readmission issue at all).[24]

Chapter 4 has shown that some of these agreements equate cases where the nationality of the person to be readmitted is 'proved', with other situations where the latter is simply substantiated or presumed *prima facie* for the purposes of the application of the agreement at hand. There are at times important variations between the accepted means of documentation for determining *prima facie* nationality—*functional identity*-of the person to be readmitted. An exception is Annex of the EURA with Pakistan which in contrast to the other five EURAs only foresees that the list of documents "shall initiate the process of establishing nationality". The comparative account of procedures and lists of documents in determining nationality reveals a largely heterogeneous and diversified picture which brings about complexity and a very high degree of heterogeneity from one agreement to another.

Differing rules on identification (and related travel documents) may add further practical obstacles to responsible authorities on the ground, which depending on who they are in each EU Member State and the third country at hand will encounter divergent set of administrative and accepted lists of documents as to who is a national of which country.[25] As shown by a study published by the EMN in 2014, the national actors responsible for implementing EURAs and issuing the readmission application vary widely across the EU Member States. Graph 5.2 shows the heterogeneity of actors and authorities involved in some EU Member States. In a majority of EU Member States the responsible authorities in the field of readmission are the police (12 Member States)[26] or the immigration authorities (11 Member States),[27] border guards (6 Member States)[28] and Ministries of Interior (5 Member States).[29] In some EU Member States more than one of these authorities share the various competences related to readmission. A more diversified picture can be expected to emerge when looking at the authorities and actors with competence or

---

[24]Peers et al. (2012).

[25]EMN (2014) Annex 2 Table A2.1.

[26]Bulgaria, Czech Republic, Estonia, Finland, Greece, Hungary, Malta, Slovakia, Slovenia, Spain and Sweden.

[27]Belgium, Cyprus, Estonia, Finland, Germany, Hungary, Ireland, Lithuania, Luxembourg, Netherlands and Sweden.

[28]Estonia, Finland, Latvia, Lithuania, Poland and Slovakia.

[29]Austria, Cyprus, Croatia, France and Germany.

powers over the identification and issuing of travel documents for purposes of readmission in third (non-EU) countries.

The comparative analysis of the six EURAs in Chap. 4 above has revealed that a key contribution of these EU legal instruments has been formalising the transmission of readmission applications through competent diplomatic and/or consular channels of the states concerned. The EURA with Pakistan constitutes an exception here. As Annex of this book illustrates, Article 2 of the agreement dealing with readmission of own-nationals does not expressly mention the role of diplomatic and consular authorities. The involvement of diplomatic/consular authorities of the third country concerned does in principle ensure that the application is no longer handled directly or solely between border, police or immigration (or Ministries of Interior) authorities of the states concerned. Rather EU authorities need to go through the diplomatic channels and Ministries of Foreign Affairs of these third countries, which often entail heavier procedures. The consequence has been that the responsible third country authorities cross-examine and verify the evidence or list of documents provided in a detailed manner. This may not only increase the time spent, but most importantly allows requested states to take into account issues which transcend EU-centric security and policing (expulsion-driven) priorities.

The de-linking of the process of determining a person's legal identity from the nationality of her/his state of origin opens up a rocky path which brings us to the ultimate shores of states' sovereignty in international relations at times of deciding who their national actually are. EURA lay down a set of rules and practices that cross dangerously the boundaries of sovereignty of the requested state for readmission at times of deciding who is a national and who is not in its national law and practice. While substantiation or *prima facie* means of proof are generally considered acceptable in the scope of EURAs examined in this book, this does prevent that the processes of identification in inter-state relations continue representing one of the most important obstacles in the operability of EURAs.

Arguably EU Member States, and by extension the EU, are behaving as if they would be entitled to re-determine the identity of people for purposes of expulsion. EURAs function as tools intended to foster third countries changes as regards how they confer their nationality and who is considered by law and practice as a national of those countries. The *Pham* case studied in Chap. 3 constitutes a case in point. The decision stands in a difficult position in light of current international standards and the interpretation of these provided by the UN High Commissioner for Refugees (UNHCR).[30] Article 1.1 of the 1954 Convention relating to the Status of Stateless Persons states that the term 'stateless person' means "a person who is not considered as a national by any State under the operation of its law". This provision has been interpreted as including both *de jure* and *de facto* statelessness. When considering the question as to whether a person is stateless, the UNHCR

---

[30]Carrera and de Groot (2015).

Guidelines[31] make a clear and specific recommendation when determining the non-possession of any foreign nationality. They underline in paragraph 19 that

> A Contracting State must accept that a person is not a national of a particular State if the authorities of that State refuse to recognize that person as a national. A Contracting State cannot avoid its obligations based on its own interpretation of another State's nationality laws which conflicts with the interpretation applied by the other State concerned.

The 2014 UNHCR Handbook on the Protection of Stateless Persons provides further clarification that in the phrase "under the operation of its law" enshrined in Article 1.1 of the 1954 Convention, the law means "not just legislation, but also ministerial decrees, regulations, orders, judicial case law (in countries with a tradition of precedent) and, where appropriate, customary practice."[32] The UK Supreme Court considered UNHCR Guidelines and Handbook to present a too broad interpretation of what "its law" actually means and concluded that there was no evidence "of a decision made or practice adopted by the Vietnamese government which treated the appellant as a non-national by operation of its law". Irrespective of these international and regional standards, the Court considered the UK Secretary of State for the Home Department entitled to carry out its own interpretation of Vietnamese nationality law and overtake the decision by Vietnamese authorities as regards who is a national in light of national legal system.

The UK Supreme Court ruling stands in a difficult relationship with the set of legal standards stemming from the jurisprudence of the CJEU in cases where EU Member States deprive an EU citizen of their nationality and therefore the status of citizenship of the Union. This is particularly so in respect of the 2010 CJEU ruling in *Rottmann v. Freistaat Bayern*,[33] where the Court held that in cases of withdrawal decisions national courts must pay due regard to the principle of proportionality.[34] The Court clarified that the national court would need to determine whether having regard to the relevant circumstances of the case at stake, the principle of

---

[31]UNHCR (2012) p. 5. See also UNHCR (2013).

[32]Ibid, p. 12. The Handbook continues by saying that "Establishing whether an individual is not considered as a national under the operation of its law requires a careful analysis of how a State applies its nationality laws in an individual's case in practice and any review/appeal decisions that may have had an impact on the individual's status.16 This is a mixed question of fact and law", Ibid.

[33]Case *Rottmann* C-135/08, ERC I-1449.

[34]In paragraph 56 of the ruling the Luxembourg Court held that "Having regard to the importance which primary law attaches to the status of citizen of the Union, when examining a decision withdrawing naturalisation it is necessary, therefore, to take into account the consequences that the decision entails for the person concerned and, if relevant, for the members of his family with regard to the loss of the rights enjoyed by every citizen of the Union. In this respect it is necessary to establish, in particular, whether that loss is justified in relation to the gravity of the offence committed by that person, to the lapse of time between the naturalisation decision and the withdrawal decision and to whether it is possible for that person to recover his original nationality."

proportionality would grant the person a "reasonable period of time in order to try to recover the nationality of his Member State of origin".[35]

As the Luxembourg Court stated in *Rottmann*, the essential criterion for the EU general principle of proportionality to be applicable in reviewing the legality of EU Member States' decisions in cases of withdrawal is not prior possession of another EU Member State nationality, or the need of a cross-border element. Instead, paragraph 42 of the *Rottmann* judgment emphasizes that the determining factor in the legality test is the extent to which the decision leaves the individual "in a position capable of causing him to lose the status conferred by Article 17 EC and the rights attaching thereto".[36] All these considerations were not properly taken into account by the UK Supreme Court, which effectively led Mr. Pham to loose not only British nationality but also European citizenship, while also leaving open the inter-state dispute as regards whose national?.

5.4 The Blurring of Rights

EURAs represent the flagship legal instrument shaping the intersection between expulsion policies and international relations in the EU. Any assessment of their implementation would remain blind without properly acknowledging and examining their impact for the agency and status of the individual[37] subject to these readmission processes. Controversially, as tools of international relations EURAs are predominantly driven and focused on the 'rights and duties' of the states' parties involved. They have been therefore designed, and studied by international relations scholars, in the context of inter-state interests and struggles. This study has illustrated how one of the key policy priorities shared by both EU Member States and the European Commission is the increase of expulsion rates of irregular immigrants present in the Union's territories. The matching of the number of removal orders and actual expulsions has been discursively framed as the turning point in ensuring the 'effectiveness' of EU's returns and readmission policy.

The EU's current obsession with returns rates not only prevents a proper discussion of the asymmetries and tensions that the practice of readmission poses to inter-state relations regarding who is a national. It also nuances and blurs one of the main reasons why people cannot be returned, i.e. their rights and entitlements as citizens and holders of fundamental human rights. The reach and margin of states' national sovereignty in the treatment of citizens and foreigners in migration regulations must remain delimited within the boundaries set by international human rights and European law standards. Several instruments composing the international human rights Treaty framework state clearly that *everyone* has the right to leave any

---

[35]Ibid. Paragraph 58.
[36]Carrera and de Groot (2015).
[37]Guild (2009).

5.4 The Blurring of Rights

country (including their own) and to return to their country. This is the case for example in Article 13.2 of the Universal Declaration of Human Rights (UNHR),[38] which was given specific form in Article 12 of the International Covenant on Civil and Political Rights (ICCPR).[39] They enshrine the individual's claim or right towards her/his country of origin or nationality.

A majority of EURAs state that after giving a positive reply to the readmission application, the competent diplomatic mission or consular office shall issue the necessary travel document "irrespective of the will of the person to be readmitted". The overlapping between readmission sovereign duties and individuals' rights and is however far from uncontested. The exact weight between the right and willingness of the individual to return and the obligation/right of the state of origin to readmit its nationals remains controversial. This dilemma was acknowledged by the Council Legal Service (CLS) back in 1999 when asked to assess the impact of the Amsterdam Treaty over Member States' competences on readmission.[40] The CLS Opinion stated that

> ... it is doubtful that in the absence of a specific agreement to this effect between the states concerned, a general principle of international law exist which would oblige those State to readmit their own nationals if they do not wish to return to their country of origin.[41]

Plender has highlighted how an increasing number of national constitutional regimes across the world are characterizing the right to enter in one's country of origin as a fundamental human right.[42] Noll raised central questions at times of assessing the relation between 'the right' of the state of destination to return irregular immigrants with the right of individuals to leave[43]: Does the individual's unwillingness to expulsion translate into a 'right not to return'? Is the protective content of human rights law beyond state interests? What remains less contested in the academic discussion is the inherent relationship between the right of individuals to leave and to return to their country with other key human rights obligations

---

[38]Article 13 UDHR reads as follows: "(1) Everyone has the right to freedom of movement and residence within the borders of each state. (2) Everyone has the right to leave any country, including his own, and to return to his country."

[39]Article 12 ICCPR states that "1. Everyone lawfully within the territory of a State shall, within that territory, have the right to liberty of movement and freedom to choose his residence. 2. Everyone shall be free to leave any country, including his own. 3. The above-mentioned rights shall not be subject to any restrictions except those which are provided by law, are necessary to protect national security, public order (*ordre public*), public health or morals or the rights and freedoms of others, and are consistent with the other rights recognized in the present Covenant. 4. No one shall be arbitrarily deprived of the right to enter his own country."

[40]Council of the EU (1999) paragraph 6.

[41]The CLS stated that "However, there exists a well-established obligation under international law for each state to readmit its own nationals if the latter wish to return. For example, Article 12.4 of the International Covenant of Civil and Political Rights provides that "No one may be arbitrarily deprived of the right to enter his own country". Footnote 3 of the Opinion.

[42]Plender (1988).

[43]Noll (1999), pp. 23–24, Noll (2003).

enshrined in international and European legal instruments.[44] They chiefly include the principle of *non-refoulement* according to which no one will be expelled, returned or extradited to a state where s/he may face a risk amounting to torture.[45] These obligations are now embedded in the EU legal system through the Treaties and Article 19 of the EU Charter of Fundamentals Rights.[46] The six EURAs under assessment include (to a variety of degrees) express references to these international human rights obligations. Usually these take the form of so-called 'Non-Affection Clauses'.

The content and scope of these provisions in EURAs have taken different forms and shapes depending on the country concerned. Some EURAs like the one with Pakistan do not provide any specific or expressly stipulated list of legal instruments that are of relevance for the application of the agreement. However, the EURA with Pakistan needs to be read in conjunction with the 2004 EC-Pakistan Cooperation Agreement (PAC) which states in Article 1 that the "respect for human rights and democratic principles as laid down in the Universal Declaration on Human Rights underpins the domestic and international policies of the Community and the Islamic Republic of Pakistan and constitutes an essential element of this Agreement." The situation concerning human rights protection in Pakistan was in fact an issue of serious concern for the European Parliament during the negotiations of the EURA.[47] The EURAs with Armenia, Azerbaijan, Cape Verde, Georgia and Turkey all include express references to and list relevant international obligations in instruments such as the Universal Declaration of Human Rights of 1966, the 1951 UN Convention on the Status of Refugees (as amended by the Protocol of January 1967) on the Status of Refugee, international conventions determining the state responsible for examining applications for asylum lodged, the UN Convention of December 1984 against Torture, or other specific instruments such as the Convention on International Civil Aviation of December 1944.

As Peers et al. have argued a large number of those persons expelled by means of a readmission agreement are likely to be asylum seekers or applicants for other forms of international protection.[48] Beyond formalistic references to human rights instruments in EURAs, the literature has highlighted and documented the international protection challenges in their operability. A particularly problematic aspect inherent to *the practice* in the readmission logic is its linkage to "the safe third country principle". According to UNHCR the safe third country concept is based on the

---

[44]Guild (2013).

[45]Refer to Article 3.1 of the UN Convention against Torture.

[46]Article 19.2 reads as follows: "No one may be removed, expelled or extradited to a State where there is a serious risk that he or she would be subjected to the death penalty, torture or other inhuman or degrading treatment or punishment." Article 18 of the Charter also stipulates that "The right to asylum shall be guaranteed with due respect for the rules of the Geneva Convention of 28 July 1951 and the Protocol of 31 January 1967 relating to the status of refugees and in accordance with the Treaty establishing the European Community."

[47]European Parliament (2004).

[48]Peers et al. (2012).

5.4 The Blurring of Rights

principle that "asylum-seekers/refugees may be returned to countries where they have, or could have, sought asylum and where their safety would not be jeopardized, whether in that country or through return there from to the country of origin".[49]

Coleman has argued that "A particular problem in the implementation of safe third country policies is that the Member State objective of minimizing the amount of persons in the asylum procedure has reduced the guarantee of safety in individual cases".[50] He has acknowledged that the wording of EURAs raises direct challenges to the rights of asylum seekers and refugees. However, the lack of specific provisions in some EURAs regarding the relationship between EURAs and safe third country principle makes it indeed difficult to pass the human rights test. The Achilles heel of EURAs from a human rights perspective is that there is not meaningful way to ensure that people with protection claims will be properly guaranteed in their implementation in the requested state.[51] This protection gap is particularly problematic in the phase of 'post-readmission' in the third country concerned. As the European Commission highlighted in 2011, a key weakness in the operability of EURA is the absence of any mechanism to monitor what happens to persons (notably TCNs) after their readmission.[52] Inter-state trust is simply not sufficient to ensure compliance. This has been confirmed by the Parliamentary Assembly of the Council of Europe (PACE) which called the EU to "instruct an appropriate body to monitor the implementation by member states of European Union-brokered readmission agreements" and to

> ensure that readmission agreements provide for a system under which the implementation of the agreement may be properly monitored and evaluated, and that they provide for a public annual report to be drawn up by the authorities of the readmitting country including, as a minimum, statistical data on the fate of readmitted persons (on issues such as detention, release, expulsion, access to asylum system, etc.).[53]

---

[49]UNHCR (1991).

[50]Coleman (2009) p. 227.

[51]Carrera and Guild (2015).

[52]European Commission (2011). The Commission stated that "It would be important to know if the third country has respected the human rights of persons after their readmission." It recommended that "The Commission should consider to launch, with the support of the External Action Service, a pilot project with one of the principal international organisations active in the migration area in a particular third country with which an EURA is in force (e.g. Pakistan or Ukraine), tasking that organisation to monitor the situation of persons readmitted under the EURA and to report back to the respective JRC. On the basis of an evaluation of this pilot project, and with due regard to human and financial resources available, the Commission could decide to extend such a project to all third countries with which EURAs have been concluded. It could also be further analysed to what extent the monitoring system of forced return as required by the Return Directive may contribute to the "post-return" monitoring in question", pp. 13 and 14.

[53]Council of Europe Parliamentary Assembly (2010). The PACE also recommended the EU to "7.3 include in its readmission agreements as a condition for their application, that an asylum seeker to whom the agreement is applied shall first have had access in the European Union member state to an effective remedy in the sense of Article 13 of the European Convention on Human Rights, and that the agreements shall not be applied until the competent authority has ruled on the asylum seeker's appeal".

In addition to issues related to international protection and asylum, EURAs fall within the scope of existing EU immigration legislative instruments providing a harmonized set of Union rules in the field of expulsion of irregular immigrants, in particular the so-called Returns Directive.[54] This Directive, as well as all the case-law developed by the CJEU since its entry into force, are of direct application to EU readmission practices and instruments. EU Member States practices in the scope of EURAs must be in accordance to, and compatible with, the set of rules and standards enshrined in this piece of EU secondary legislation, and the subsequent jurisprudence by the Luxembourg Court. Among all the EURAs examined, only the EURA with Turkey makes express reference in the scope of Article 18 (Non-Affection Clause) to the need for the Agreement to comply with the rights and procedural guarantees in this Directive as well as other relevant legal instruments composing the current state of EU migration and asylum law.

The Returns Directive has received ample criticism in the academic literature due to its predominant focus on ensuring swift 'return'.[55] Recital 4 of the Directive establishes as one of its objectives "Clear, transparent and fair rules need to be fixed to provide for an effective return policy as a necessary element of a well-managed migration policy". Still, this Directive now sets a supranational framework of standards, procedural guarantees and rights subject to judicial scrutiny by the CJEU. This 'supranationalisation' has been understood to have displayed rather positive effects over the rights of irregular immigrants in the EU, in particular concerning the procedural remedies and time-limits concerning detention.[56] The Returns Directive envisages a set of procedural guarantees for TCNs which in practice may legitimately delay the actual expulsion procedure, chiefly the right to an effective remedy.[57] These circumstances are not deemed as 'obstacles' towards the effectiveness of the Directive. Rather, they are understood as a key way to ensure its legitimate, fair and effective functioning.

Article 13 of the Returns Directive foresees that irregular migrants must have an effective remedy to appeal against or seek review of decisions related to return before an independent competent judicial or administrative authority, "or a competent body composed of members who are impartial and who enjoy safeguards of independence." The appeals body must have the power to suspend the enforcement

---

[54]Directive 2008/115/EC of the European Parliament and of the Council of 16 December 2008 on common standards and procedures in Member States for returning illegally staying third-country nationals, OJ L 348, 24.12.2008, p. 98.

[55]Baldaccini (2009), Acosta Arcarazo (2012), Mitsilegas (2015) pp. 93–107.

[56]Peers et al. (2012).

[57]Peers et al. (2014). Article 47 of the EU Charter of Fundamental Rights states that "Everyone whose rights and freedoms guaranteed by the law of the Union are violated has the right to an effective remedy before a tribunal in compliance with the conditions laid down in this Article. Everyone is entitled to a fair and public hearing within a reasonable time by an independent and impartial tribunal previously established by law. Everyone shall have the possibility of being advised, defended and represented. Legal aid shall be made available to those who lack sufficient resources in so far as such aid is necessary to ensure effective access to justice".

5.4 The Blurring of Rights

of return decisions. The Directive also foresees that the third country national needs to have access to legal advice, representation and when necessary linguistic assistance. As long as the suspensory effect of the review by an independent authority is taking place the 'postponement of removal' is justified. Article 9 adds that EU Member States may postpone removal when it would violate the principle of *non-refoulement* or "for an appropriate period taking into account the specific circumstances of the individual case" and taking into account: "the third-country national's physical state or mental capacity and, technical reasons, such as lack of transport capacity, or failure of the removal due to lack of identification."[58]

Pending removal, third country nationals are holders of a set of 'safeguards pending return' stipulated in Article 14 of the Directive. This provision emphasizes that EU Member States shall ensure that the following principles are taken into account: maintenance of family unit with family members present in their territory, provision of emergency health care and essential treatment of illness, access to basic education by minors and take into account special needs of vulnerable persons. According to the EU Returns Handbook drafted by the Commission in 2015, "The returnee is, however, not considered to be legally staying in a Member State, unless a Member State decides—in accordance with Article 6.4—to grant a permit or a right to legal stay to the returnee". Article 6.4 of the Returns Directive provides EU Member States with the option to granting a residence permit "compassionate, humanitarian, or other reasons". Recital 12 of the Directive further proclaims that EU Member States should provide non-removable persons with a written confirmation of their situation.[59]

Peers (2015) has studied how the CJEU rulings interpreting the various provisions embodying the Returns Directive have attempted to 'balance' the often contradictory goals of ensuring the humane treatment of irregular migrants, with the objective of expelling irregular migrants as soon as possible. The Court has clarified the scope of detention in light of the Directive's obligation to grant voluntary departure,[60] or the implementation of the right to be heard (as part of the right of

---

[58]According to the EU Returns Handbook published by the European Commission in 2015 "The catalogue of possible reasons is open and allows Member States to react flexibly to any newly arising or newly discovered circumstances justifying postponement of removal. The concrete examples listed in the Return Directive (physical or mental state of the person concerned; technical reasons, such as lack of availability of appropriate transport facilities) are indicative examples. Member States may provide also for further cases in their national implementing legislation and/or administrative practice", p. 50. European Commission (2015).

[59]Recital 12 of the Directive reads as follows "The situation of third-country nationals who are staying illegally but who cannot yet be removed should be addressed. Their basic conditions of subsistence should be defined according to national legislation. In order to be able to demonstrate their specific situation in the event of administrative controls or checks, such persons should be provided with written confirmation of their situation. Member States should enjoy wide discretion concerning the form and format of the written confirmation and should also be able to include it in decisions related to return adopted under this Directive."

[60]See for instance CJEU Cases C-61/11 (PPU) *El Dridi* 28 April 2011; C-554/13 *Zh. & O.* 11 June 2015; C-146/14 (PPU) *Mahdi* 5 June 2014.

good administration enshrined in Article 41 the EU Charter of Fundamental Rights) in the context of return and detention decisions. EU Member States are obliged to issue a removal order and enforce it, or regularize the individual involved.[61] The CJEU concluded in case *Mahdi* C-146/14,[62] that despite Article 6.4 and Recital 12, EU Member States are not obliged to issue an autonomous residence permit or other authorization conferring the right to stay

> …to a third-country national who has no identity documents and has not obtained such documentation from his country of origin, after a national court has released the person concerned on the ground that there is no longer a reasonable prospect of removal within the meaning of Article 15(4) of that directive. However, that Member State must, in such a case, provide the third-country national with written confirmation of his situation.[63]

The current policy priority paid by EU institutional instances on increasing returns rates irrespective of the proper implementation of these administrative and legal (including human rights) safeguards for individuals in the process of expulsion is thus problematic. As the Recital of the Returns Directive expressly mentions, testing effectiveness in return procedures must go hand-to-hand clear, transparent and fair rules, in full compliance with the fundamental human rights of irregular immigrants which may *de jure* prevent people to be returned irrespective of the existence of a removal order. Legal certainty, proportionality and fundamental rights are not just 'technical barriers' and cannot go at the expense of inter-state interests on migration control. The European Union Agency for Fundamental Rights (FRA) (2011) has provided a detailed account of the reasons preventing removal based on human rights considerations. These include considerations related to the protection of family and private life, medical and health conditions, humanitarian situations in the country of origin and best interests' considerations. It is therefore regrettable that the 2016 Council Conclusions.

Measuring effectiveness in implementation when comparing removal orders and returns is of a limited value for understanding the effects of EURAs. The goal of increasing return rates in comparison to the total number of removal orders does not address effectiveness from the perspective of the extent to which there are in fact too many removal orders being issued for people whom the competent national authorities know for a fact are not expellable. Expulsion orders may be taken

---

[61]The CJEU ruled in the case *Zaizoune* ruling that "…where a return decision has been issued against a third-country national, but that third-country national has not complied with the obligation to return, whether within the period for voluntary departure, or if no period is granted to that effect, [the Directive] requires Member States, in order to ensure the effectiveness of return procedures, to take all measures necessary to carry out the removal of the person concerned, namely, … the physical transportation of the person concerned out of that Member State", paragraph 33. C-38/14 *Zaizoune* 23 Apr. 2015. Furthermore, in the case *Kadzoev* (Case C-357/09 PPU), the Court concluded in paragraph 63 that "detention ceases to be justified and the person concerned must be released immediately when it appears that, for legal or other considerations, a reasonable prospect of removal no longer exists."

[62]C-146/14 (PPU) *Mahdi* 5 June 2014.

[63]Ibid. Paragraph 89.

perhaps too lightly by relevant authorities at domestic levels without carefully looking at the information available in individual cases and passing it to migration enforcement authorities while there are procedures or appeal processes still pending. Moreover, return decisions are often not final in nature; especially in those cases where those concerned are contesting the legality of their removal order. Finally, the equation of removal orders and enforced return decisions is over-simplistic. It does not take into account that the administrative status of individuals is not something fixed in stone or static in nature. There is nothing existential about irregularity. The legal status or circumstances of those subject to a removal order may change over time, and the person may cross the bridge toward regularity of stay or residence. The EURA procedures constitute an attempt to artificially fixate or 'freeze' the individual into a migratory status of irregularity.

Open Access This chapter is distributed under the terms of the Creative Commons Attribution 4.0 International License (http://creativecommons.org/licenses/by/4.0/), which permits use, duplication, adaptation, distribution and reproduction in any medium or format, as long as you give appropriate credit to the original author(s) and the source, a link is provided to the Creative Commons license and any changes made are indicated.

The images or other third party material in this chapter are included in the work's Creative Commons license, unless indicated otherwise in the credit line; if such material is not included in the work's Creative Commons license and the respective action is not permitted by statutory regulation, users will need to obtain permission from the license holder to duplicate, adapt or reproduce the material.

References

Acosta Arcarazo D (2012) The good, the bad and the ugly in EU migration law: Is the European Parliament becoming bad and ugly? (The adoption of the directive 2008/115: the returns directive). In: Guild E, Minderhoud P (eds) The first decade of EU migration and asylum law. Martinus Nijhoff Publishers, Leiden, pp 179–205

Baldaccini A (2009) The return and removal of irregular migrants under EU law: an analysis of the returns directive. Eur J Migr Law 11(1):1–71

Bouteillet-Paquet D (2003) Passing the buck: A critical analysis of the readmission policy implemented by the European Union and its Member States. Eur J Migr Law 5:359–377

Carrera S, de Groot GR (eds) (2015) European citizenship at the crossroads: the role of the European Union on loss and acquisition of nationality. Wolf Legal Publishers, Oisterwijk

Carrera S, Guild E (2014) The European Council's guidelines for the Area of Freedom, Security and Justice 2020: subverting the 'Lisbonisation' of justice and home affairs?. CEPS Essay, Brussels

Carrera S, Guild E (2015) Can the new refugee relocation system work? Perils in the Dublin logic and flawed reception conditions in the EU. CEPS Policy Brief, Brussels

Cassarino JP (2010) Readmission policy in the European Union. Study for the European Parliament, Brussels

Coleman N (2009) European readmission policy. Third country interests and refugee rights, Martinus Nijhoff, Leiden

Council of Europe Parliamentary Assembly (2010) Readmission agreements: a mechanism for returning irregular migrants. Do. 12168, Strasbourg, Rapporteur: Tineke Strik

Council of the EU (2002) Criteria for the identification of third countries with which new readmission agreements need to be negotiated. 7990/02, Brussels, 16 Apr 2002

Council of the EU (1999), Standard readmission agreement between the member states of the EU, of the one part, and a third country, of the other part—Impact of the entry into force of the Treaty of Amsterdam, 6658/99, 10 Mar 1999

European Commission (2011) Evaluation of EU readmission agreements. COM (2011) 76, 23 Feb 2011

European Commission (2013) Communication on the work of the task force Mediterranean. COM (2013)869, 4 Dec 2013

European Commission (2015) Recommendation establishing a common "Return Handbook" to be used by Member States' competent authorities when carrying out return related tasks. C (2015) 6250, 1 Oct 2015

European Migration Network (EMN) (2014) Good practices in the return and reintegration of irregular migrants: member states' entry bans policies and use of readmission agreements between member states and third countries. European Commission, Brussels

European Parliament (2004) Report on the proposal for a council decision on the cooperation agreement between the European Community and the Islamic Republic of Pakistan on partnership and development. C5-0659/2001, 20 Apr 2004

European Union Agency for Fundamental Rights (FRA) (2011) Fundamental rights of migrants in an irregular situation in the European Union. Publications Office of the European Union, Luxembourg

Goodwin-Gill GS (1975) The limits of the power of expulsion in public international law. Brit Yearb Int Law 47(1):55–156

Gregou M (2014) Drawing the geographical boundaries of expulsion and readmission in Greece: the dynamics of an elusive process. Eur J Migr Law 16(4):505–533

Guild E (2013) The right to leave a country. Issue Paper by the Council of Europe Human Rights Commissioner, Strasbourg

Guild E (2009) Security and Migration in the 21st Century. Polity Press, Cambridge

Guiraudon V (2000) European integration and migration policy: vertical policy-making as venue shopping. J Common Mark Stud 38(2):251–271

Hailbronner K (1997) Readmission agreements and the obligation on states under public international law to readmit their own and foreign nationals. Zeitschrift für ausländisches öffentliches Recht und Völkerrecht 57:1–49

Kruse I (2006) EU readmission policy and its effects in transit countries: The case of Albania. Eur J Migr Law 8(2):115–142

Mitsilegas V (2015) The criminalisation of migration in Europe: challenges to human rights and the rule of law. Springer, London

Noll G (1999) Rejected asylum seekers: the problem of return. New Issues in Refugee Research, Working Paper 4, UNHCR, Geneva

Noll G (2003) Return of persons to state of origin and third states. In: Aleinikoff TA, Chetail V (eds) Migration and international legal norms. T.M.C Asser Press, The Hague, pp 61–74

Peers S et al (2012) EU immigration and asylum law (text and commentary) 2nd edn. Volume 2: EU immigration law. Martinus Nijhoff Publishers, Leiden

Peers S et al (2014) The EU charter of fundamental rights: a commentary. Hart Publishing, Oxford

Peers S (2015) Irregular migrants: Can humane treatment be balanced against efficient removal? Eur J Migr Law 17(4):289–304

Plender R (1988) International migration law. Martinus Nijhoff Publishers, Leiden

Singleton A (2016) Migration and asylum data for policy-making in the European Union. CEPS Liberty and Security Series in Europe, Brussels

References

UK House of Commons (2013) EU readmission agreement with Armenia. European Scrutiny Committee, London, 9 Jan 2013

UNHCR (1991) Background Note on the safe country concept and refugee status. EC/SCP/68, 26 July 1991

UNHCR (2012) Guidelines on statelessness No. 4—Ensuring every child's right to acquire a nationality through Articles 1-4 of the 1961 Convention on the reduction of statelessness. HCR/GS/12/04, Geneva, 21 Dec 2012

UNHCR (2013) Expert Meeting interpreting the 1961 statelessness convention and avoiding statelessness resulting from loss and deprivation of nationality. Summary Conclusions, Geneva

UNHCR (2014) Handbook on protection of stateless persons. Geneva. http://www.unhcr.org/53b698ab9.pdf Accessed 21 May 2016

Chapter 6
Conclusions

This book has identified and critically examined the implementation challenges of EURAs. The efficiency and legitimacy of EU and its Member States' expulsion policies are being currently tested by several EU institutional instances from the perspective of enforced return rates as a percentage of the number of removal orders being issued. On this basis, a number of policy initiatives have been put forward by the European Commission in order to increase the return rates of EU Member States. These include: first, enhancing the role of Frontex in supporting EU Member States in identifying and coordinating Joint Return (Flights) Operations to countries of origin; second, the development of biometric technologies and ensuring interconnections between national and EU/international databases; third, the adoption of a new EU travel document featuring higher technical and security standards; and fourth, the development of informal (non-legally binding) working arrangements on readmission with third countries.

It has shown that none of these EU proposals would satisfactorily address one of the most fundamental challenges facing the implementation of EURAs after their entry into force. A comparative analysis of six EURAs has shown that these legal instruments aim at establishing common rules, procedures and lists of documents seeking to facilitate the identification and removal of nationals to their countries of origin. While much attention has been paid in scholarly discussions to the dilemmas posed by the inclusion in EURAs of an obligation to readmit third-country nationals and stateless persons, a major point of controversy in the functioning of EURAs is the processes of identification (and subsequent issuing of travel documents by the relevant authorities of the requested state) of the nationality of the person to be readmitted.

The practical obstacles in the identification of own nationals to be readmitted raise far-reaching challenges which substantiate why removal orders cannot always be enforced by relevant authorities. These are summarised below.

First, EURAs trespass the sovereign boundaries of the requested third country in defining or assuming the nationality of the individual to be expelled. They foresee a number of rules and lists of documents used for determining nationality but which do not constitute irrefutable or complete proof of the nationality of the person. Instead, they presume substantiation of a 'functional identity' of the individual for the purposes of the application of EURAs irrespective of what the nationality legislation (law and practice) of the assumed country of origin specifies about who is or is not a national.

The controversy in the implementation or quasi-suspension of the EURA with Pakistan, or national cases such as *Pham v. Secretary of State for the Home Department* in the UK, illustrate the ongoing disagreements and kind of open questions that arise between states, and between the EU and third countries, over the legality of decisions determining legal identity of persons in the context of readmission policies. They also stand in constant friction with international and EU standards and principles limiting the margin of manoeuvre enjoyed by states and EU actors at times of documenting or determining the nationality of an individual, or in matters related to the withdrawal or deprivation of nationality.

Second, the nature of EURAs as tools of international relations relegate a proper focus of their effects over the agency and rights of individuals affected by readmission logics. The current EU's obsession in increasing return rates blinds the fact that another key reason why people cannot be expelled is due to the obligations by EU Member States to guarantee their rights and entitlements as fundamental human rights holders stemming from the EU legal system. EURAs are now subject to the rights and guarantees foreseen by EU immigration and asylum legislation, such as those enshrined in the EU Returns Directive, as well as the judge-made standards and principles developed by the Luxembourg Court.

These standards ultimately recognize the need for irregular immigrants to have access to fair and effective remedies and good administration in relation to removal orders. This includes the fundamental right to appeal against a removal order before independent national authorities with the power to suspend the enforcement of expulsion. EU law guarantees also prevent the removal of individuals in cases where there is no guarantee of compliance with the principle of *non-refoulement*, on the basis of individual and fundamental rights (humanitarian, personal or family) circumstances or where practical obstacles (such as the lack of identification or travel documents) exist preventing removal.

The identified implementation challenges are further exacerbated by the lack of effective monitoring mechanisms to ensure proper and independent accountability of the ways in which concluded EURAs function. This is particularly so in respect of their implementation or post-readmission practices in third states, or in cases where EU agencies such as Frontex are involved through Joint Return Flights. The currently envisaged rules of Implementing Protocols or decisions adopted by Joint Readmission Committees in each of the EURAs, which remain confidential, fall short in ensuring the necessary level of transparency, democratic accountability and legal certainty in their practical application. The last written evaluation by the European Commission on the functioning of EURAs was issued in 2011. An objective and independent assessment of the value added of EURAs is equally jeopardized by the lack of accurate EU statistics regarding the nature, scope and effects of expulsions practices, and their relationship with EURAs.

Measuring the effectiveness of EURAs and EU expulsion policies on the basis of increasing the return rates puts the EU and its Member States in an existential conundrum: fastening and easing the enforcement of removal orders through readmission instruments opens up frictions with international and EU legal principles and standards applicable to the determination of who is a national of which state; the readmission logic also blurs the legal status of irregular immigrants as holders of fundamental rights and administrative guarantees envisaged in EU law and the EU Charter of Fundamental Rights. Proper compliance of inter-state and inter-personal standards are in turn central at times of ensuring humane, fair, human rights compliant and legitimate migration policies. These standards demand for expulsion rates to be ineffective.

This conundrum illustrates a deeper illusion[1] that the state—and the EU by default—can in fact effectively manage cross-border human mobility, and prevent irregular migration, irrespective of the agency of the individual. The implementation or practical obstacles examined in this book, which are inherent to the EURA logic in expulsion processes, might ultimately help us to understand why EU Member States have been so keen in calling and putting reiterated pressures on the European Commission to conclude EURAs with third countries. EURAs fail in overcoming the practical barriers to expulsion experienced at Member States' arenas. They reveal a policy universe where national and EU actors intersect, compete and engage in 'blame-shifting games' over the ineffectiveness of expulsion policies.

The more recent EU policy priorities to move towards informal EU readmission arrangements and non-legally binding instruments may be read as an attempt by EU institutional instances and actors to find 'the soft spot' in third countries' authorities which will be willing to cooperate on the readmission of the persons concerned outside existing venues and instruments subject to public, democratic and judicial accountability. In this way, EU external migration law and policy become an example of 'venue shopping'. EU actors use or attribute new informal uses to readmission instruments and search for new fields of collaborations in an attempt to avoid legal (rule of law) constraints and find new co-operating parties or new allies in third countries.

These informal policy instruments and venues do not properly address, and may even exacerbate, the challenges in practical implementation related to the identification of own nationals which have been identified and studied in this book. EU readmission instruments lacking legal certainty and blurring individuals' fundamental rights contravene the EU's rule of law and fundamental rights foundations. They also undermine the credibility of the EU's readmission policy. Assessing the effectiveness of EU migration policies must go beyond narrow numerical accounts of expulsion rates and the current policy obsession on increasing returns of irregular immigrants. For their legitimacy and value added to endure, EU policies must go firmly hand-to-hand with humane, fair and rights-compliant standards.

---

[1]Bigo (1996, 2005).

The analysis provided in this book reveals the complexities underlying the implementation dynamics of EU external migration law and policies and the external dimensions of the European Agenda on Migration. EURAs constitute one example of the wider toolbox of policy, legal and financial instruments delineating domestic and EU actors cooperation venues with third countries in the management of migration. The research findings substantiate the need for developing new theoretically grounded understandings of the foreign affairs-migration policy nexus which move beyond pure policy-transfer, implementation and instrumentation literature. The dynamics characterizing EU readmission policies show the need to pay attention to intersecting policy universes around which various (EU and third country) authorities and actors make use of legal and policy instruments according their interests, and the ways in which they relate, compete and collaborate when dealing with the inefficiencies inherent to irregular migration policies. Who are the main actors setting priorities, framing the agenda and using different instruments in the domains of migration, asylum and borders? Who benefits from the 'external dimensions of the European Agenda on Migration' and what are the main power dynamics and struggles at stake? How can we understand the complex and fragmented field of venues and multi-instruments framing EU's relations with third countries on migration policies? This book has revealed how formal and informal readmission instruments and fields show frictions and present challenges escaping democractic rule of law and fundamental human rights of individuals.

Open Access This chapter is distributed under the terms of the Creative Commons Attribution 4.0 International License (http://creativecommons.org/licenses/by/4.0/), which permits use, duplication, adaptation, distribution and reproduction in any medium or format, as long as you give appropriate credit to the original author(s) and the source, a link is provided to the Creative Commons license and any changes made are indicated.

The images or other third party material in this chapter are included in the work's Creative Commons license, unless indicated otherwise in the credit line; if such material is not included in the work's Creative Commons license and the respective action is not permitted by statutory regulation, users will need to obtain permission from the license holder to duplicate, adapt or reproduce the material.

References

Bigo D (1996) L'illusoire maîtrise des frontières. Le Monde Diplomatique 511:9–10
Bigo D (2005) Frontier controls in the European Union: Who is in control? In: Bigo D, Guild E (eds) Controlling frontiers: free movement into and within Europe. Ashgate Publishing, Aldershot, pp 49–99

Annex

Detailed Comparative Overview of EURAs

This Annex provides a comparative overview of the EURAs with Pakistan, Georgia, Armenia, Azerbaijan, Cape Verde and Turkey. The sequence of countries follows a chronological order in light of their entry into force. The table contains direct extracts or quotes from the Agreements. The Annex offers an in-depth account of the main similarities and differences in these six EURAs in relation to:

- Preamble (A.1)
- Main definitions (A.2)
- General provisions (A.3)
- Readmission obligations (own-nationals) (A.4)
- Readmission procedures (principles and means of evidence regarding nationality) and time limits (A.5–A.7)
- Affection clauses (A.8)
- Implementation and application (A.9); and
- Annexes.

	Pakistan	Georgia	Armenia	Azerbaijan	Cape Verde	Turkey
A.1. Preamble	"This Agreement shall be without prejudice of the rights, obligations and responsibilities of the Member States of the European Union and Pakistan under international law"	Ibid. and "in particular, from the European Convention of 4 November 1950 for the Protection of Human Rights and Fundamental Freedoms (ECHR) and the Convention of 28 July 1951 on the Status of Refugees as amended by the Protocol of 31 January 1967"	Ibid.	Ibid. "In particular, from the Convention of 28 July 1951 on the Status of Refugees and its Protocol of 31 January 1967"	Ibid. and "in particular, from the Convention of 28 July 1951 on the Status of Refugees" "Having regard to the Joint Declaration of 5 June 2008 on a Mobility Partnership between the European Union and Cape Verde, in accordance with which the Parties will take steps to develop a dialogue on the readmission of persons without authorisation with a view to ensuring effective cooperation for their return"	Ibid. "In particular, from the European Convention of 4 November 1950 for the Protection of Human Rights and Fundamental Freedoms and the Convention of 28 July 1951 on the Status of Refugees" "This Agreement shall be without prejudice to the rights and procedural guarantees for persons who are subject to return procedures in or who apply for asylum in a Member State as laid down in the respective legal instruments of the Union" "This Agreement shall be without prejudice to the provision of the Agreement of 12 September 1963 establishing an Association between the European Economic Community and Turkey, its additional protocols, the relevant Association Council decisions as well as the relevant case-law of the Court of Justice of the European Union, EMPHASISING that the persons holding a long term residence permit granted under the terms of Council Directive 2003/109/EC concerning the status of third-country nationals who are long-term residents enjoy a reinforced protection against expulsion under Article 12 of that Directive"

(continued)

Annex 69

(continued)

	"National of Pakistan shall mean any person who holds the nationality of Pakistan" (Article 1.c)	"National of Georgia shall mean nay person who holds the citizenship of Georgia" (Article 1.b)	National of Armenia shall mean any person who holds the citizenship of Armenia in accordance with the legislation of the Republic of Armenia (Article 1.b)	"National of Azerbaijan shall mean any person which holds the citizenship of Azerbaijan in accordance with its legislation" (Article 1.d)	"National of Cape Verde shall mean any person with Cape Verde nationality" (Article 1.b)	"National of Turkey shall mean any person who holds the nationality of Turkey in accordance with its legislation"
A.2. Definitions						
A.3. General provisions	N.A.	N.A.	FUNDAMENTAL PRINCIPLES: "the Requested and Requesting State shall ensure respect for human rights and for the obligations and responsibilities following from relevant international instruments; The Requested State shall ensure the protection of the rights of persons readmitted to its territory; The Requesting State should give preference to voluntary return over forced return (Article 2)"	FUNDAMENTAL PRINCIPLES: Ibid. (Article 2)	N.A.	SCOPE: Article 2.1: "The provisions of this Agreement shall apply to persons who do not or who no longer, fulfil the conditions for entry to, presence in, or residence on the territories of Turkey or one of the Member States of the Union 2. The application of the present Agreement, including Paragraph 1 of this article, shall be without prejudice to the instruments enumerated in Article 18 (Non-Affection Clause) 3. The present Agreement shall not apply to third country nationals or stateless persons as referred to Articles 4 and 6 who have left the territory of the Requested State more than five years before the Requesting State's competent authorities has gained knowledge of such persons unless the conditions required for their readmission to the Requested State as stipulated by Articles 4 and 6 can be established by means of documents enumerated in Annex 3"

(continued)

(continued)

A.4. Readmission obligations Own nationals	Readmission of nationals	Readmission of Nationals	Readmission of own nationals	Readmission of own nationals	Readmission of own nationals	Readmission of own nationals
	Article 2	Article 2	Article 3	Article 3	Article 2	Article 3
	"The Requested State shall readmit, after the nationality having been proved in accordance with Article 6, upon application by the Requesting State any of its nationals who does not, or who no longer fulfils the conditions in force for entry into, presence in, or residence on, the territory of the Requesting State"	"Upon application by a Member State and without further formalities other than those provided for in this Agreement". "provided that it is proved, or may be validly assumed on the basis of prima facie evidence furnished, that they are nationals of Georgia"	Ibid.	Ibid	Ibid. "Pursuant to Article 13.5.c.i of the Cotonou Agreement…"	Ibid. "it is established that they are nationals of Turkey"
	Refer to Joint Declaration concerning Article 2.1 according to which "The Parties take note that, according to the current Pakistan Citizenship Act, 1951, and the Rules made thereunder, a citizens of Pakistan cannot renounce his citizenship without having acquired or having been given a valid document assuring the grant of citizenship or nationality of another State. The Parties agree to consult each other as and when the need arises"	"2. Georgia shall also readmit (a) minor unmarried children of the persons mentioned in paragraph 1…; and (b) spouses, holding another nationality, of these same persons"	Ibid. "Spouses holding another nationality or who are stateless"	Ibid.	Ibid.	Ibid. "Spouses, holding another nationality"
		"3. Georgia shall also readmit persons who have been deprived of, or who have forfeited or renounced, the nationality of Georgia since entering the territory of a Member State, unless such persons have at least been promised naturalisation by that Member State"	"3. Armenia shall also readmit persons who have renounced the nationality of Armenia since entering the territory of a Member State, unless such persons have at least been promised naturalisation by that Member State"	"3. Azerbaijan shall also readmit persons, illegally present or residing in the Requesting Member State who have renounced the nationality of Azerbaijan in accordance with the national laws of the latter since entering the territory of a Member State…"	"3. Cape Verde shall readmit persons who have been deprived of, or who have renounced, the nationality of Cape Verde since entering the territory…"	3. Ibid. "…have been deprived of or who have renounced…"

(continued)

Annex

(continued)

2. The Requested State shall, as necessary and without delay, issue the person whose readmission has been accepted with the travel document required for his or her readmission, which shall be valid for at least six months If, for legal or factual reasons, the person concerned cannot be transferred within the period of validity of the travel document, the Requested State shall issue a new travel document with the same period of validity within 14 days"	4. After Georgia has given a positive reply to the readmission application, the competent diplomatic mission or consular office of Georgia shall, irrespective of the will of the person to be readmitted, immediately and no later than within 3 working days, issue the travel document required for the return of the person to be readmitted with a period of validity of 90 days. If Georgia has not, within 3 working days, issued the travel document, it shall be deemed to accept the use of the EU standard travel document for expulsion purposes"	4. Ibid. "[…]. immediately, free of charge and no later than within three working days…issue the travel document required for the return of the person to be readmitted with a period of validity of 120 days"	4. Ibid. "…free of charge and no later than five working days, issue the travel document required for the return of the person to be readmitted with a period of validity of 150 days. If Azerbaijan does not, within five working days, issue the travel document,…"	4. "[…] Immediately and no later than within four working days issue the travel document…for a period of validity of six months" If Cape Verde has not, within four days, issued the travel document, it shall be deemed to accept the use of the Union standard travel document for expulsion purposes"	"or, where appropriate, after expiry of the time limits laid down in Article 11.2" "within three working days, issue the travel document required for the return of the person to be readmitted with a period of validity of three months" "the reply to the readmission application shall be considered as the necessary travel document for the readmission of the person concerned"
	"5. If, for legal or factual reasons, the person concerned cannot be transferred within the period of validity of the travel document that was initially issued, the competent diplomatic mission or consular office of Georgia shall, within 3 working days, extend the validity of the travel document or, where necessary, issue a new travel document with a period of validity of the same duration. If Georgia has not, within 3 working days, issued the new travel document or extended its validity, it shall be deemed to accept the use of the EU standard travel document for expulsion purposes"	5. Ibid. "[…] and free of charge" *Joint Declaration concerning Articles 3.3 and 5.3: "The Contracting Parties take note that, according to the nationality laws of the Republic of Armenia and the Member States, it is not possible for a citizen of the Republic of Armenia or the European to be deprived of his or her nationality. The Parties agree to consult each other in due time should this legal situation change"	5. Ibid. "within five working days" *Joint Declaration concerning Article 3.3: "The Contracting Parties take note that, according to the nationality laws of the Republic of Azerbaijan, it is not possible for a citizen of the Republic of Azerbaijan to be deprived of his or her nationality. The Parties agree to consult each other in due time, should this legal situation change" *Joint Declaration concerning Articles 4 and 6: "The Parties will endeavour to return any third country national who does not, or who no longer, fulfils the legal conditions for entry to, presence or residence to his/her country of origin"	5. Ibid. "within four working days" *Joint Declaration concerning Articles 3 and 5: "The Contracting Parties will endeavour to return any third country national who does not, or who no longer, fulfils the legal conditions in force for entry to, presence in or residence on their respective territories, to his or her country of origin"	5. Ibid. "within three working days" "…..the reply to the readmission application shall be considered as the necessary travel document for the readmission of the person concerned"

(continued)

(continued)

A.5. Readmission procedure Principles	Article 4 Submission of Readmission Application to competent authority	Article 6	Article 7	Article 7	Article 6	Article 7
	"No readmission application needed when the person holds a valid travel document or a valid visa/residence authorisation of the Requested State"	Ibid. "or identity card"	Ibid "a valid visa or residence permit"	Ibid.	"(a) in the case of the requested States' own nationals, if the person to be readmitted holds a valid travel document or identity card"	Ibid.
	"2. …nationals valid travel document …third country nationals and stateless persons also a valid visa or residence permit of the Requested State…" Ibid.					3. Ibid. "nationals travel document or identity card…" "The previous sub-paragraph shall not prejudice the right of the relevant authorities to verify at the border the identity of the readmitted person"
	"No person shall be readmitted only on the basis of prima facie evidence of nationality"	N.A.	N.A.	N.A.	N.A. (b) in the case of third country nationals or stateless persons, if the person was apprehended at the airport of the requesting State after having arrived directly from the territory of the requested State"	N.A.
		"3. …if a person has been apprehended in the border region (including airports) of the Requesting State after illegally crossing the border coming directly from the territory of the Requested State, the Requesting State may submit a readmission application within 2 days following the persons apprehension (*accelerated procedure*)"	Ibid.	"3. Without prejudice to paragraph 2, if a person has been apprehended in an area which extends up to 15 km from and including the territories of seaports and international airports, including custom zones, of the Requesting State after illegally crossing the border, coming directly from the territory of the Requested State, the Requesting State may submit a readmission application within two working days following that person's apprehension (*accelerated procedure*)"	"3. "third country nationals and stateless persons holding a valid travel document and a valid visa or residence permit issued by the requested State, the transfer shall require only the written notification from the requesting State to the competent authority" 4. "written notification shall be necessary in the case of the transfer of any person requiring an escort" 5. "border region" Ibid.	On accelerated procedures see Article 7.4 (Ibid.) "if a person has been apprehended by the Requesting State in the border region after having entered illegally and directly from the territory of the Requested State…" NEW: "1. The Member States and Turkey shall make every effort to return a person referred to in Articles 4 and 6 directly to the country of origin. For this purpose, the modalities of the application of this Paragraph shall be determined in accordance with point (b) of Article 19 (1). The provisions of this

(continued)

Annex

(continued)

| | | | | | Paragraph shall not apply to cases in which the accelerated procedure is applicable in accordance with Paragraph 4 of this Article" Joint Declaration on Article 7 (1): "The Parties agree that in order to demonstrate 'every effort to return a person referred to in Articles 4 and 6 directly to the country of origin', the Requesting State, while submitting a readmission application to the Requested State, should at the same time submit a readmission application also to the country of origin. The Requested State shall reply within the time limits mentioned in Article 11(2). The Requesting State informs the Requested State if a positive reply to the readmission application has been received from the country of origin in the meantime. In case where the country of origin of the person in question could not be determined and therefore a readmission application could not be submitted to the country of origin, the reasons of this situation should be stated in the readmission application which will be submitted to the Requested State" |

(continued)

(continued)

	Article 6	Article 8	Article 9	Article 8	Article 9
A.6. Readmission procedures Means of evidence regarding nationality	"1. Evidence cannot be furnished through false documents""	N.A. (see below)	N.A. (see below)	N.A. (see below)	N.A. (see below)
	"2. Proof of nationality may be furnished through any documents listed in Annex I to this Agreement, even if their period of validity has expired. If such documents are presented, the Requested and the Requesting States shall mutually recognise the nationality without further investigation being required" "3. Proof of nationality may also be furnished through any of the document listed in Annex II to this Agreement, even if their period of validity has expired. If such documents are presented the Requested State shall initiate the process for establishing the nationality of the person concerned"	Ibid. "…including documents the validity of which has expired by up to 6 months" Ibid. "prima facie evidence…" NEW: "If such documents are presented, the Member States and Georgia shall deem the nationality to be established, unless they can prove otherwise". "Prima facie evidence of nationality cannot be furnished through false documents"	Ibid. "can be particularly furnished…." "Proof of nationality cannot be furnished through false documents" Ibid. Ibid.	Ibid. Ibid.	1. "…If such documents are presented, the Member States or Turkey respectively shall for the purpose of this Agreement, recognise the nationality" Ibid. NEW: "shall deem for the purpose of this Agreement, the nationality to be established, unless following an investigation and within the time limits laid down in Article 11, the Requested state demonstrates otherwise"
	"4. If none of the documents listed in Annexes I and II can be presented, the competent authority of the Requesting State and the diplomatic or consular representation of the Requested State shall make arrangements to interview the person for whose readmission an application has been submitted, without undue delay"	Ibid. "or if they are insufficient…shall, upon a request from the Requesting State which is included in the readmission application…." "…at least within 4 working days from the date of receipt of the readmission application, in order to establish his or her nationality. The procedure for such interviews may be	Ibid. "at least within five working days from the date of receipt of the readmission application"	Ibid. "at least within three working calendar days of the date of the request…"	Ibid. "within seven working days" NEW: "In case there are no diplomatic or consular representations of the Requesting State in the Requesting State, the former shall make the necessary arrangements in order to interview the person to be readmitted without undue delay, at the latest within

(continued)

(continued)

			established in the implementing Protocols provided for in Article 19 of this Agreement"				seven working days from the requesting day. The procedure for such interviews may be established in the implementing Protocols provided for in Article 20 of this Agreement"
A.7. Readmission procedures Time limits	Article 8		Article 10	Article 11	Article 10	Article 11	Article 11
	"1. Readmission application submitted to the competent authority of the Requested state within a maximum of one year"		Ibid. "within a maximum of 6 months"	Ibid. "within a maximum period of 9 months"	Ibid. "Within a maximum of 6 months"	Ibid. "within a maximum of one year"	Ibid. "Within a maximum of 6 months"
	"...where there are legal or factual obstacles to the application being submitted on time, the time limit shall, upon request, be extended but only until the obstacles have ceased to exist"		Ibid.	Ibid.	Ibid.	Ibid.	Ibid.
	"2. A readmission application must be replied to without undue delay, and in any event within a maximum of 30 calendar days. Reasons shall be given for refusal of a readmission application"		Ibid. "in writing: (a) within 2 working days if the application has been made under the accelerated procedure; (b) within 12 calendar days in all other cases"	Ibid.	Ibid. "(b) fifteen calendar days in all other cases	Ibid.	Ibid. "– within five working days if the application has been made under the accelerated procedure... – without undue delay, and in any event within a maximum of 25 calendar days in all other cases..."
			NEW: "reasons for refusal shall be given in writing" (Article 10.3)	Ibid.	Ibid.	Ibid.	Ibid. (Article 11.4)
					NEW: "Replies to readmission applicants may be sent by any means of communication, including by electronic means or fax"	Ibid.	Ibid.

(continued)

(continued)

	"This time period begins to run from the date of receipt of the readmission application"	Ibid. NEW: "If there is no reply within this time limit, the transfer shall be deemed to have been agreed to"	Ibid.	Ibid.	Ibid.	Ibid.
	"Where there are legal or factual obstacles, the time limit lay be extended up to 60 calendar days. Where there is no reply within this time limit, the transfer shall be deemed to have been agreed to"	N.A.	N.A.	N.A.	N.A.	N.A.
	"3. After agreement has been given, or upon expiry of the above-mentioned time limit, the person concerned shall be transferred within three months. Upon request, this time limit may be extended by the time taken to deal with legal or practical obstacles"	Ibid.	Ibid.	Ibid.	Ibid.	Ibid.
	Article 15 *Consistency with other legal obligations*	Article 17 *Non-affection clause*	Article 18 *Relation to other international obligations*	Article 18 *Relation to other international obligations*	Article 17 *Without prejudice clause*	Article 18 *Non-affection clause*
A.8. Non-affection clause/other international obligations	"1. This Agreement shall be without prejudice to the rights, obligations and responsibilities of the Community, the Member States and Pakistan arising from or under international law, and international treaties to which they are Parties"	Ibid.	Ibid.	Ibid.	Ibid.	Ibid.
		"(a) The Convention of 28 July 1951 on the Status of Refugees as amended by the Protocol of 31 January 1967 on the Status of Refugee"	Ibid. (Article 2)	Refer to Article 2 Fundamental Principles)	Ibid.	Ibid.

(continued)

Annex   77

(continued)

		"(b) the international conventions determining the State responsible for examining applications for asylum lodged"	Ibid.	Ibid.	Ibid.
		"(c) the European Convention of 4 November 1950 for the Protection of Human Rights and Fundamental Freedoms, and its Protocols"	Ibid. (Article 2)	Refer to Article 2	Ibid.
		"(d) the UN Convention of 10 December 1984 against Torture and other Cruel, Inhuman or Degrading Treatment or Punishment"	Ibid. (Article 2)	Refer to Article 2	"the Convention of 10 December 1984 against Torture and other Cruel, Inhuman or Degrading Treatment or Punishment"
		"(e) international conventions on extradition and transit"	Ibid.	Ibid.	Ibid.
		"(f) multilateral international conventions and agreements on the readmission of foreign nationals, such as the Convention on International Civil Aviation of 7 December 1944"	Ibid. (no express reference to the Convention)	Ibid.	Ibid.
					"where applicable, the European Convention of 13 December 1955 on establishment" "2. The present Agreement shall fully respect the rights and obligations provided by the 1963 EU-Turkey Association Agreement, its additional Protocols, the relevant Association Council decisions as well as the relevant case-law of the Court of Justice of the EU" NEW: See paragraphs 3-6 "Nothing in this agreement

(continued)

(continued)

				shall be without prejudice to the rights and procedural guarantees of persons: *being subject of return procedures (Directive 2008/115) "in particular with regard to their access to legal advice, information, temporary suspension of the enforcement of a return decision and access to legal remedies *applying for asylum (Directive 2003/9 and Directive 2005/85), "in particular with regard to the right to remain in the Member State pending the examination of the application *holding a long term residence permit under Directive 2003/109 *granted residence under Directive 2003/86 on the right to family reunification"
"2. Nothing in this Agreement shall prevent the return of a person under other bilateral arrangements"	Ibid.	Ibid. NEW: "under other formal or informal arrangements"	Ibid.	Ibid.
"3. This Agreement shall be without prejudice to the remedies and rights available to the person concerned under the laws of the host country including international law"	N.A.	Ibid.	Ibid.	Ibid.

(continued)

(continued)

A.9. Implementation and application	Article 16 *Joint Readmission Committee* The Parties shall provide each other with mutual assistance in the application and interpretation of this Agreement. To this end, they shall set up a Joint Readmission Committee (hereinafter referred to as the Committee) which will, in particular, have the task of:	Article 18 Ibid.	Article 19 Ibid.	Article 18 Ibid.	Article 19 Ibid.
	"(a) monitoring the application of this Agreement;"	Ibid. "…necessary for the uniform application of this Agreement"	Ibid. "and exchange of information…excluding personal data"	"(a) Monitoring the application of this Agreement"	Ibid.
			"(b) to address issues arising out of the interpretation or application of the provisions of this Agreement"	N.A.	"(b) to decide on implementing arrangements necessary for the uniform application of this Agreement"
	"(b) deciding on technical arrangements necessary for its uniform execution, including amendments to Annexes III and IV"	"…on implementing arrangements…"	Ibid.	Ibid.	N.A.
	"(c) having a regular exchange of information on the implementing Protocols drawn up by individual Member States and Pakistan pursuant to Article 17"	N.A.	Ibid.	Ibid.	Ibid.
	"(d) proposing amendments to this Agreement and Annexes I and II"	Ibid.	Ibid.	Ibid.	Ibid.
	"2. The decisions of the Committee shall be taken by unanimity and be implemented accordingly."	"2. The decisions of the Committee will be binding on the Contracting parties"	Ibid.	Ibid.	NEW: "2. The decisions of the committee shall be binding on the Contracting Parties following any necessary internal procedures required by the law of the Contracting Parties"

(continued)

"3. The Committee shall be composed by representatives of the Community and Pakistan. The Community shall be represented by the European Commission, assisted by experts from Member States"	Ibid.	Ibid.	Ibid.	Ibid.
"4. The Committee shall meet where necessary at the request of one of the Parties, normally on an annual basis"	Ibid.	Ibid.	Ibid.	Ibid.
"5. Disputes which cannot be resolved by the Committee shall be settled through consultations between the Parties"	N.A.	N.A.	N.A.	N.A.
"6. The Committee shall establish its rules of procedure, including establishing a working language common to both Parties"	Ibid.	Ibid.	Ibid.	Ibid.
Article 20 *Implementing Protocols*	Article 19	Article 20	Article 19	Article 20
1. Pakistan and a Member State may draw up an implementing Protocol which shall cover rules on:	"1. On the request of a Member State or Georgia, Georgia and a Member State shall draw up an implementing Protocol…"	"1. Without prejudice to the direct applicability of the present agreement…"	Ibid.	"1. On the request of a Member State or Turkey, Turkey and a Member State shall draw up an Implementing Protocol…."
(a) the designation of the competent authorities, the border crossing points and the exchange of contact points	Ibid.	Ibid.	Ibid.	Ibid.
"(b) the conditions for escorted returns, including the transit of third country nationals and Stateless persons under escort"	Ibid.	Ibid.	Ibid.	Ibid.

(continued)

Annex

(continued)

	"(c) means and documents other than those listed in the Annexes I to IV to this Agreement"	Ibid.	Ibid.	Ibid.	Ibid. "(c) evidence and documents…"	Ibid.
		"(d) the modalities for readmission under the accelerated procedure"	Ibid.	Ibid.	Ibid. "(d) the arrangements for readmission under the accelerated procedure"	Ibid. "(d) the modalities for readmission under the accelerated procedure"
		"(e) the procedure for interviews"	Ibid.	Ibid.	Ibid.	Ibid.
		"2. The implementing Protocols shall enter into force only after the Committee has been notified"	Ibid.	Ibid.	Ibid.	"2. The implementing Protocols referred to in Paragraph 1 shall enter into force only after the readmission committee has been notified"
		NEW: "3. Georgia agrees to apply any provision of an implementing Protocol drawn up with one Member State also in its relations with any other Member State upon request of the latter"	Ibid. "The Member States agree to apply any provision of an implementing Protocol concluded by one of them also in their relations with Armenia upon request of the latter, subject to practical feasibility of its application to other Member States"	Ibid. Following model in EURA with Armenia	Ibid. Following model in EURA with Georgia	N.A.
Annex I	Common List of documents the presentation of which is considered as evidence of nationality	Common List of documents the presentation of which is considered as proof of citizenship	Common List of documents the presentation of which is considered as proof of nationality	Common List of documents the presentation of which is considered as proof of nationality	Common List of documents the presentation of which is considered as proof of nationality	Common List of documents the presentation of which is considered as proof of nationality
	"Genuine Passports of any kind (national passports, diplomatic passports, service passports, collective passports and surrogate passports including children's passports)"	Ibid. (the word 'genuine' has been omitted)	Ibid.	Ibid.	Ibid.	Ibid.

(continued)

(continued)

	"– Computerised national identity cards"	Ibid. (the word 'Computarised' omitted)	Ibid. "including temporary and provisional ones"	Ibid. "with the exception of seaman's identity cards"	Ibid.	Ibid.
	"– Genuine citizenship certificates"	Ibid. (the word 'genuine' has been omitted): "and other official documents that mention or clearly indicate citizenship"	Ibid.	N.A.	"Nationality certificates and other official documents that mention or clearly indicate nationality"	"Citizenship certificates and other official documents that mention or clearly indicate nationality"
				"laissez-passer issued by the requested State"	Ibid.	Ibid.
					"service books and military identify cards" "seamen's registration books and skippers' service cards"	"military service books and military identify cards" "seamen's registration books and skippers' service cards"
					"confirmation of identity as a result of a search carried out in the Visa Information System (VIS)/In case of Member States not using VIS, positive identification established from the visa application records kept by those Member States"	Ibid.
Annex II	Common list of documents the presentation of which shall initiate the process of establishing nationality	Common list of documents, the presentation of which is considered as *prima facie* evidence of nationality – Documents listed in Annex I, the validity of which as expired by more than 6 months	Common list of documents, the presentation of which is considered as *prima facie* evidence of nationality Ibid.	Common List of Documents, the presentation of which is considered as *prima facie* evidence of nationality – Documents listed in Annex I, the validity of which as expired by more than 6 months	Common List of Documents, the presentation of which is considered as *prima facie* evidence of nationality N.A.	Common List of Documents, the presentation of which is considered as *prima facie* evidence of nationality Ibid. "whose validity has expired"
	"– Digital fingerprints or other biometric data"	N.A.	N.A. Only "Fingerprints"	N.A. "Fingerprints"	N.A. Only "Fingerprints"	N.A.
	"– temporary and provisional national identity cards, military identity cards and birth certificates issued by the Government of the Requested Party"	"– birth certificates or photocopies thereof/service books and military identity cards"	Ibid. than Pakistan	Ibid.	Ibid. than Georgia	"Birth certificates or photocopies"

(continued)

Annex

(continued)

"– photocopies (officially authenticated by the authorities of Pakistan) of other official documents that mention or indicate citizenship (e.g. birth certificates)"	"– Photocopies of any of the documents listed in Annex I"	Ibid.	Ibid.	Ibid.
"– service cards, seaman's registration cards, skipper's service cards or photocopies thereof"	Ibid.	Ibid.	N.A.	N.A.
"– Statements made by the person concerned"	Ibid. "…and language spoken by him or her, including by means of an official test result"	Ibid. "statements by witnesses"	Ibid. (including the features of the previous three EURAs)	Ibid. "written account of statements made by the person concerned and language spoken by him or her, including by means of an official language test"
	"– Driving licences or photocopies thereof"	N.A.	"Driving licences or photocopies"	Ibid.
	"– Company identity cards or photocopies thereof"	Ibid.	Ibid.	Ibid.
	"– Any other document which may help to establish the nationality of the person concerned"	Ibid.	Ibid.	Ibid.
	"– Laissez passer issued by the Requested State"	Ibid.	N.A.	Ibid. "including documents with pictures issued by the authorities in replacement of the passport"
	"– Confirmation of identity search carried out in the Visa Information System (VIS)/In the case of Member States not using the VIS, positive identification established from visa application records"	Ibid.	Ibid. "Confirmation of identity search carried out in IAMAS (Entry-Exit and Registration Automated Information Search System"	N.A.	See above

The Table applies the following legend:
N.A.: Non applicable/Not included
Idem: Similar/Included
"..": New sentences and paragraphs
NEW: New sentences and paragraphs of particular relevance

Printed in the United States
By Bookmasters